DRYFIRE

DRYFIRE

Fundamental Shooting Techniques for Training at Home

BEN STOEGER

Foreword by Andreas Yankopolus

Skyhorse Publishing

Skyhorse Publishing books may be purchased in bulk at special discounts for sales promotion,
corporate gifts, fund-raising, or educational purposes. Special editions can also be created to
specifications. For details, contact the Special Sales Department, Skyhorse Publishing,
307 West 36th Street, 11th Floor, New York, NY 10018 or info@skyhorsepublishing.com.

Skyhorse® and Skyhorse Publishing® are registered trademarks of Skyhorse Publishing, Inc.®,
a Delaware corporation.

Visit our website at www.skyhorsepublishing.com.

Please follow our publisher Tony Lyons on Instagram @tonylyonsisuncertain.

10 9 8 7 6 5 4 3 2 1

Library of Congress Cataloging-in-Publication Data is available on file.

Print ISBN: 978-1-5107-7939-6
eBook ISBN: 978-1-5107-7940-2

Cover design by David Ter-Avanesyan
Cover photograph by Getty Images

Printed in China

CONTENTS

FOREWORD

I got into competitive shooting by tagging along with a friend to shoot an IDPA match in 1999. The results were ugly, but I loved the challenge and came back for more, joining the club so I could practice on weekends. I knew I needed help and took a few classes, which got me squared away on the fundamentals of marksmanship. These were the kinds of classes where everyone stands on the shooting line and blasts a target at five or ten yards. Practicing that material got me to Expert, but I couldn't make progress beyond that—I simply didn't see what I should do differently or how shooting faster was possible. That stagnation eventually got the better of me, and I dropped out of IDPA in 2005.

I kept up casual pistol shooting and fiddled with AR-15s and precision rifles for a few years until the desire to compete got me shooting Steel Challenge in 2011. This put me in the company of several USPSA shooters who encouraged me to give that sport a try because I was finishing well in local Steel Challenge matches.

My USPSA shooting got off to a rough start. I landed in A class four months after shooting my first match based on my Steel Challenge skills. I then shot the 2013 Georgia Championship a few weeks later and came in 48th, which carried the distinction of low A. You don't get a trophy or cash payout for that kind of finish! What happened? I could hit the "A" zone just fine, and my shooting pace wasn't terrible for A class, but it took me forever to move between positions and reload. And what was this shooting on the move thing people were telling me I needed to do? That's what you get when you jump from Steel Challenge to USPSA.

Right before the championship, Ben had taught a class at my home range. It was already full, but Ben said he'd happily teach another one if I'd round up a goon squad. We're talking Area 6 here, so finding goons wasn't a problem. The class was on. Maybe Ben would chase me with an axe to provide the sense of urgency I needed?

I had read Ben's books by the time the class rolled around, but it was still a revelation. For starters, I got to see world-class shooting close up. Ben first shot each drill or sample stage, then we tried, with Ben quickly assessing each student's skill level and providing individualized feedback and coaching. Ben cleverly designed the sample stages and drills to complement each other. If a drill involved shooting on the move, the next stage would reward shooting on the move. If the drill positioned targets at a wide range of distances, the stage would feature a shooting position with a similar target arrangement. This helped us both recognize and execute a variety of shooting challenges in context.

For me, Ben's individualized feedback weighted heavily toward moving and shooting more rapidly, often with comical results. One drill had us run forward to a fault line and shoot three targets at seven yards. My first attempt was at the speed of a brisk walk. Ben called out: "Again, but run this time!" I ran to the fault line and skidded to a stop like a car with locked-up wheels, giving everyone a good laugh. Ben then patiently worked with me on coming into position with finesse. No easy task. Sometimes Ben's feedback came in a style all his own. I'll never forget hearing "Is that all you got?" in response to shooting a drill—that axe wouldn't have encouraged me as much!

We all got sent home with a clear sense of where we needed to focus our practice efforts along with recommended livefire and dryfire drills to run. It was time to get to work!

Dryfire was interesting at the time as we lived in an 800-square-foot condo with hardwood floors. I turned our 12-foot by 14-foot bedroom into my dryfire ludus. Our queen-sized bed was pressed against one wall, which gave me a U-shaped path for moving between shooting positions and flipping magazines onto the mattress when performing reloads. For targets, I initially stuck Post-it® notes on the walls and doors until the Pro Shop started selling scaled cardboard IPSC ones. "We're being invaded by little men," joked my wife. More like a small army after setting up 32-round field courses.

But even in that small space, I burned thousands of reps into my subconscious, pushed myself to ratchet down par times on standard drills, and learned how my grip, stance, draws, reloads, and movement should feel when done correctly. Not having the distraction of the gun going off let me put my full attention on gripping the gun, processing and refining the sight picture, and running the trigger when things looked good.

When I wanted to alter something about my shooting, I'd first spend a few evenings in dryfire grooving in the new technique so it would be partially programmed into my subconscious when I hit the range to try it with live ammunition. These livefire results would guide my dryfire for the next week. This training regimen hasn't changed as I've progressed in my skills, experimented with different shooting techniques, and received guidance from better shooters.

Dryfire most evenings and live practice most weekends got me to M class just in time for the 2014 Georgia Championship, where I finished 11th and happily didn't win low M. Coming this far from 48th the previous year shows just what dedication to Ben's personalized training plan can accomplish.

The year closed out with a move to a house with a basement, where I finished a 22' x 14' section as my dedicated dryfire ludus and reloading area. This larger practice space lets me freely work position entry/exit drills without having to navigate a bed and fling magazines without having to worry about damaging furniture or the floor—and crank out lots of 9mm for practice and matches.

I was fortunate to train with Ben a few more times, where he evaluated my progress, corrected aspects of my shooting, and gave me an updated training plan. Ben was hardly standing still himself, always working to improve his shooting and teaching techniques to stay on top of his game. To me, his progress has been particularly evident in how he's taught movement and body positioning while flowing through the shooting positions of a stage.

The 2015 and 2016 shooting seasons saw me crack the "Top 10" at the Georgia Championship, which has gotten progressively more demanding in the Atlanta-area Production shark tank—I'm not the only one upping their game thanks to all the classes Ben has taught in the Atlanta area. GM also looks within striking distance with my classification at 93 percent at the start of 2017. (2024 update: I made GM in 2017 and snagged a couple of state championships and podium finishes—including GA Production Champion [Overall]—in subsequent years.)

I know my weaknesses and have drills in place to chip away at them in dryfire and livefire. Unlike feeling lost when I threw in the towel with IDPA, I've never felt more excited about pistol shooting than today, because I know it's within my power to improve. Work hard and intelligently and you can do the same!

—Andreas Yankopolus

MY DRYFIRE JOURNEY

When I got interested in shooting competitively, my real concern was about training. I didn't have any money at the time and ammo cost a *lot*. I had a gun; I just didn't have access to a stockpile of ammo in order to get good with the gun. This isn't an uncommon problem. Most people are more regulated by their budgets than by their motivation.

As I was learning about IDPA and USPSA, I was most interested in finding out how to get good. Looking at the available materials and opinions online at the time, I found many answers to the "How do I get good?" question. One answer was that how good you get is predetermined by how much cash you have for ammo. Another answer is that your skills are determined by how old you are or how talented you are. Another answer was that you could dryfire. There were some guys that were doing dryfire practice for multiple hours in a single day. I learned that I could practice pretty much everything to do with shooting, except recoil control, just by doing dryfire. If I wanted to get good, I could, and dryfire was the way to do it.

I immediately bought all the training material on the market. I also read all the internet forums available at that time. I then devised my dryfire training. I had scaled targets and a timer and the whole works. My apartment became a dryfire training area. I was doing it hours a day. I was running 30-round dryfire

stages indoors. My first season of shooting matches was very successful. I started winning club matches with my Beretta and earned a GM card. I had fired very few rounds in my life at that point. Only a few thousand, but it was working.

Over the years, I increased my involvement in the sport. I attended bigger and bigger matches and even won some of them. I got more and more money for ammo and I shot a bit more every year. Even during all that, I maintained a schedule of regular and strict dryfire training.

I started teaching other people to shoot and one of the most important parts of that was teaching them to practice. I found that in many cases it is easier to make a point or demonstrate a problem to someone if you are doing it without using ammunition. People can actually see what is happening.

In my own practice, I still dryfire as hard as ever. I have learned that simply shooting more rounds doesn't make you better. You need to diagnose and solve problems. That process is in many ways easier when you aren't shooting actual ammunition.

In any event, I have spent my adult life learning about how I can practice better and how other people can as well. This material has been tested on thousands of people. I am confident it will work for you as it has worked for me.

WHAT'S NEW IN THIS BOOK

Dryfire is one of those things that everyone knows they should be doing, but very few people take the time to do. Of that group, even fewer take the time to do it right. The whole point of this manual is to help you organize your dryfire training and maximize your potential.

This obviously isn't my first dryfire manual. I put together a "15 Minute Dryfire Program" on my website back in 2009. In 2012, I coauthored a book with Jay Hirshberg based on that system called "Guaranteed Results in 15 Minutes a Day." The first edition of *Dryfire* came onto the market in early 2014. I have conducted a number of training seminars (several hundred) in the intervening time as well, with dryfire being a regular topic of conversation and instruction. Based on this feedback from all those iterations, I have arrived at this current incarnation.

This book makes the most changes from earlier versions that I ever have.

The most obvious and important change is the way things are organized. I have this book divided into a few sections. The basic skill blocks are called "elements." Think of an element as an isolation exercise. You work on only one thing at a time. Trigger control, draws, transitions, movements, and other elements can all be most easily worked on when worked on by themselves. I have another section of "scenarios," where multiple elements are combined in common ways. Think about combining movement with target transitions or movement with reloads. These are things you will see in every match. There are also "standards" that are known distance and time drills. These are the places where I emphasize a specific time limit so you can get an idea of how fast you need to be to be competitive. Things like being able to shoot the famous "El Prez" in a specific time are important if you want to be competitive at larger matches. Finally, I have a series of fun shooting exercises that don't fit cleanly in any section, but will help prepare you for competition.

These organizational changes happened organically as I saw what was working the best in my shooting classes. Isolating one element at a time worked the best for the largest number of people. Working on movement from one spot to another, without even pulling the trigger and just observing the sight picture, was a useful training tool. I made the same steps with target transition training and draw training. The results have been positive. I want the organization and nomenclature in the book to reflect what I am doing in the classes because this book doubles as a homework manual for my USPSA Fundamentals class.

I have also added emphasis in the drills for where you should be seeing mistakes happen. I have come to the conclusion that if every repetition of your dryfire training "looks good" to you then you aren't doing it right. Commonly, people end up slowing everything down in order to made it "good" and the net result is that they do their dryfire practice unrealistically slow and don't end up correcting mistakes that happen at match pace. This is something I want to add in notes to hopefully avoid.

I have also made physical organizational changes to this book. I have now accompanied every drill diagram with a place for you to make notations about your own training. This is a logical step for this book and I hope you make use of it. I have also formatted things so each drill diagram, procedure, and log will all be accessible without having to flip pages around. Prior versions of my dryfire material have always been constructed so they will work for the vast majority of living situations. Many people live in homes without basements or backyards where they can handle a gun. I have always wanted to construct things so you don't need a basement to do dryfire training. Prior movement drills have required little space to actually execute, and I have always wanted to minimize setup time for additional targets and target scenarios. In this version, I have decided to write the drills the way I want to write them and let you adapt them for your own living situation. I realize this isn't going to be an entirely popular move, but I feel it needs to be done. The fact is, if you want to practice running longer distances (10 yards or so) with a gun in hand, it is going to be almost impossible for most people to do that in their own home. I want to give you the training tools. If you need to do them at a shooting range, that's better than not doing them at all. Feel free to adapt this material for your own training space and living situation. My hope is you can make most of it work for you.

THIS ISN'T EASY

If you are new to dryfire as a concept, then this book may seem a bit overwhelming to you. There are a multitude of drills, along with demanding standards for performance. The training material in this book is designed to produce the best shooters possible. If this seems over your head, take a deep breath and go one little drill at a time.

In order to use this book to maximum effect, you need to have a good grasp of USPSA rules and procedures, how your gun works, and a basic understanding of shooting technique. If you don't have that basic foundation, this book may go a bit over your head. Don't worry about that, just try to catch up.

Your first priority should be to find a safe place in your house to do your dryfire training on a daily basis. You will want some space to move around and some targets to "shoot" at. You will need dummy rounds. You will need a timer. Take the time to gather all of these items and get the logistics of your dryfire training sorted out before you really get going with your training.

Feel free to try some of the drills without any time limit. You can modify the drills to your liking. Feel free to just get comfortable with your gun. Once you get that stuff down, then you can start your serious training. There is no need to overwhelm or frustrate yourself right away.

Your practical shooting training is something that you will probably spend a good bit of time doing. You will probably be involved in shooting for several years. Don't feel like you need to absorb everything right away.

All of that having been said, proper training requires that you actually put in some effort. You will get calluses on your hands. You will get frustrated. You will get tired. You will dryfire on days you don't feel like doing dryfire. That is, you will do all those things if you actually want to get better and you apply yourself to your training. This is hard work; there is no way around it.

Part 1
ALL ABOUT DRYFIRE

The Goal

Obviously, you need to have a goal. What exactly should you be trying to accomplish with all this dryfire stuff? I think it would be helpful to be more specific than to just say "get better." Get better how? Specifically, what should you be able to do?

In *Skills and Drills*, I set forth the following as the minimum standard of what your dryfire training needs to do for you:

1. When you draw the gun from the holster, you get the same grip every time. You can't work with an inconsistent grip in livefire. It just isn't going to do the job.

2. You need to be able to look at any given spot, then draw the pistol and aim at that spot while having the sights show up in near-perfect alignment. This is referred to as "index" or "natural point of aim" or some variation on that. This is a very important skill to possess. You simply must be able to "drive" the gun to where you want it on a subconscious level.

3. As a logical progression of drawing the pistol with the sights aligned, you must be able to look from spot to spot and have your sights show up in alignment on that spot.

4. All gun handling skills, such as drawing and reloading, must be done smoothly and efficiently.

5. You must be able to pull the trigger straight to the rear, without disturbing the sight alignment.

Those minimum things are going to happen easily, usually within two weeks of beginning to do regular dryfire training. Aside from trigger control (item 5), most people have the basics down very quickly. This comes just from basic familiarization with your gun and your gear. I estimate that more than 85 percent of the shooters in my classes can look at a spot and draw to it with the sights aligned. This really isn't much of an ask in my opinion. Being able to pull the trigger straight back takes a bit more work, but it is certainly doable. A good way to think about the minimum standards is that you are subconsciously competent with the basics. If you want to shoot something, you just look at it, draw your pistol, and shoot it. You don't need to think your way through where to put your hands or anything like that. You think and then do.

That first step of being able to shoot without thinking through the steps really is just a first step. Once you can do it, you will want to learn how to do it better or do it faster. That's where years of training will come in. With very little training, any monkey can draw a pistol and shoot a target. If someone works at it awhile, they can draw and shoot that target in under a second. If they work at it regularly and work at it hard, they can do it under pressure, in a match, in under a second. If you methodically approach the skills in this book, you can learn to do all the drills on command, repeatably, under pressure.

Before you get too excited, I need to caution you. In order to become a well-rounded shooter, you will need to do more than just dryfire. For serious shooters, regular livefire training is absolutely needed. The minimum standard that you need to bring to this book is the following:

1. You need to livefire enough that you understand what it feels like to shoot the gun.
2. You should be able to execute fundamental techniques with live rounds. Things like proper grip, trigger control, and safe handling. You don't need to be particularly good, but you need to be competent.
3. You need to identify problems in your shooting. In many ways, your livefire training will validate your dryfire training. However, if you make mistakes in your dryfire training and build bad habits, you need to identify those habits during livefire. You can then work to correct those things in a dryfire environment.

Why Dryfire?

It seems almost redundant or somehow unnecessary to make an argument for the efficacy of dryfire training. After all, you already bought the book didn't you? But still, most people that buy this book will never really use it. That's just human nature. I think people like the idea of getting better and on some level feel that dryfire is going to help them. They know it worked for this one guy at the club and he is A class after only eight months of shooting. They may know all that stuff, but they still need it demonstrated to them on some level. They get it . . . they just aren't truly sold on actually buckling down and doing the work.

I have found the best way to truly make someone want to dryfire is to have them experience tangible performance gains. This isn't that hard in an instructional setting. I can simply make the person do dryfire while I watch and make sure it is done properly. After a few minutes, they are usually going to experience a real skill level gain on whatever element they were working on. This is something you can do yourself at home; you just need to force yourself to do the work.

Another important thing to point out is that training, without actually shooting your gun, can give you an excellent demonstration of what it is you are actually doing. Maybe you are pulling the trigger sideways and the sights are moving around like crazy. Maybe you come in to a position with your gun way down low and are unable to get that first shot off quickly. When you are doing dryfire training, you aren't going to be distracted by the noise and blast of the gun. In a way, you will see more; all you need to do is pay attention.

I have also done a number of experiments where I train people either livefire only, dryfire only, or a combination of both. In every test, the superior training method has been a combination of live and dryfire. It helps the most people, the fastest. I am not telling you not to livefire . . . I know that you will livefire. That is a given. I am telling you that a bit of dryfire is the most efficient way to improve.

The bottom line is this:

If you want to get really good, dryfire is part of the equation.

Part 2
DRYFIRE LOGISTICS

This section exists to explain how the ins and outs of dryfire training work. You need to understand how to scale targets, how to use dummy ammo to give your gun and magazines proper weight, and what things to focus on during your training.

Before I address how to use the drills in this book, we need to briefly discuss safety (because of the lawyers). The operative word in dryfire is *dry*. No live ammo. I recommend that you do not have live ammunition anywhere near your dryfire practice area. Further, I recommend that you have a safe backstop for your dryfire practice, just in case a live round somehow works its way into the mix. This means that basements are an ideal place for dryfire in many respects. If you don't have a basement, recognize that a solid wall is your best bet. You want to position things so that an accidental discharge for one reason or another is an embarrassing learning experience, not a fatal mistake.

Drill Construction

These drills are designed to be set up in a variety of living situations. You will see the word *simulated* in front of every distance that I stipulate. This is for good reason. I don't expect very many people have 10 yards of dryfire space. Virtually nobody has 25 yards. You need to simulate these distances using miniature targets. Targets are commonly available in anything from 2/3 scale to 1/4 scale. By scaling the actual distance down, you are able to create the proper effect. In order to properly scale a drill, you must multiply the target scale by the distance you wish to simulate.

Example: Simulated 10 yards with 1/4 scale targets, means you multiply 10 by 1/4. You then stand 2.5 yards from the targets (or 7.5 feet if you prefer).

I must caution you, going too small on targets can be an issue. When you make the targets extremely small, you can end up being so close to the actual target that it is difficult to pull your eye back to your front sight. The distance that this phenomenon appears at varies from person to person, but I would try to stay about five feet from the actual target, regardless of scale.

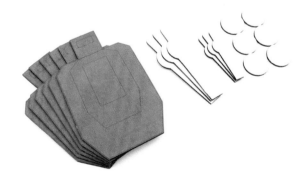

Dryfire targets are available for purchase online; this example is from the Ben Stoeger Pro Shop.

You will also see some drills that require you to set up the targets in an almost random fashion. In these situations, I do not want you to just use an "El Prez" target array. Feel free to change things up! A random setup of course is not repeatable, but then again that isn't the point.

Get a Timer

The one piece of gear that you shouldn't compromise on is a proper timer. Don't use some bullshit smart phone app; use a dedicated device. Sure, it may be loud, but you can put something over the speaker to muffle it or buy one with an adjustable volume. The simple fact is that the phone apps tend to not work terribly well. There are often issues with the accuracy of the par times. Get a legit timer. It is worth the investment.

"Firing" Multiple Shots

With a **double-action pistol**, such as a CZ or a SIG, you should pull the trigger all the way (double action) for the first shot, and then not let the trigger out far enough for it to reset. For follow-up shots, simply pull the trigger again. The trigger will not have any real resistance for the follow-up shots. When you reload or move from spot to spot, be sure to pull your finger out of the trigger guard; your first shot after that will be in double action mode.

With a **single-action pistol**, such as a 1911/2011, you only get one pull of the trigger. The rest of the time you press back on an inactive (or "dead") trigger.

With a **striker-fired pistol**, such as a Glock, you can place a rubber band into the ejection port of the gun, with the goal of holding the gun slightly out of battery. If you do this appropriately, the trigger will not be able to release the striker, so the trigger will feel a bit squishy during dryfire practice.

With any of these pistols, you will be using the trigger differently than you would if the gun were being fired live. Unfortunately, there is no good solution for this. Focus on putting pressure on the trigger and directing the pressure straight back into the frame of the gun. If you can do that consistently, you will be well on your way to good shooting.

One thing that I think should be mentioned here is that when you are pressing a "dead" trigger, you should press the trigger *hard*. This provides a good simulation for how you will usually press your trigger during actual live-fire. When people are fighting recoil, the tendency is to press hard, so you want to simulate that tendency during dryfire and learn to press the trigger straight.

Setting the Par Time

Most of these drills require that you use a par time. On many of the drills, you are required to set the par time yourself. The reason for this is twofold. First, many of the drills are tough to replicate with much consistency. This in turn makes it impossible to put down a par time and have it be very meaningful. Next, by setting the par time yourself, you should be able to set it better (in many respects) than it can be set for you.

The way it works is that, you figure out your par time for some defined action. This will not be too difficult after you work with the drills in the book for a while. Soon, you will know that it takes you about X time to engage Y targets at Z distance. With just a little bit of scenario-specific tweaking, you will very quickly nail down a time that you can repeatedly hit. As soon as you figure out your par time, follow the instructions of the drill.

During all of this, remember that a properly set par time doesn't mean "as fast as you can possibly go." You should be able to see some sort of sight picture on everything. You should be exercising appropriate care with your trigger control. On the other hand, a properly set par time doesn't mean that you hit it 100 percent of the time. It doesn't work that way. If you make a mistake, you will either not make the par time, "fire" a poor shot, or both. Remember this, if you make the par time every repetition without fail, then you are laying back too much and you need to kick it up a notch.

Prop Requirements

These drills require an absolute minimum of props. Little things like a table and a chair are required for some of the drills. Most drills only require a few targets on the wall. The most extensive prop that is used is a barricade. I prefer to use a full-size target stand with targets stapled to it to make my own barricade. You can cut an "A" zone out of a target to make that barricade into a wall with a port. I consider these props to be absolutely minimal and

the drills are designed to keep things simple. If you spent the cash to acquire this book, then you have the means to construct these drills.

Keep It Real

It can't be repeated often enough. You must remember that you are training to fire real rounds from a live gun. Train yourself to grip the gun firmly. Watch the position of the sights at all times. If you don't feel as though you have adequate control of the gun during livefire shooting, you need to figure out what technical changes you need to make and incorporate them into your dryfire. Do you want to change your arm position? Grip more firmly? Adjust your hand position? Figure it out and make it part of your training routine.

Acceptable Accuracy for Dryfire Training

You should consider acceptable accuracy in dryfire to be the same as livefire. All alpha hits aren't really a requirement of good dryfire. You want as many "A"s as possible, but because of the speeds I am encouraging you to practice at, I don't feel that every single shot needs to be perfect. Over the course of time, you should be able to score better and better points in your dryfire training. It will just take some time to achieve that.

What does it mean to "Master" a Drill?

Often, people ask me if they should move on from a drill after they have "mastered" it. "Mastering" a drill is a problematic idea. You can certainly become proficient with a drill. You can gain the skill to consistently nail the drill under the goal time. That doesn't mean that you are perfect; it just means you have the ability to perform the drill at adequate level. To be a real master, you should understand what the drill is trying to teach you and understand how the drill accomplishes that, in addition to being able to perform the drill at a high level.

Part 3

HOW DRYFIRE FITS IN YOUR OVERALL PLAN

Training Loop

What I am going to describe here is the typical training paradigm for most USPSA/IPSC/IDPA shooters that actually practice. Of course, most people don't practice, but if you do, you will likely follow this pattern.

Most of the people training shoot matches on a biweekly basis or roughly a biweekly basis. Some people only shoot a match once a month. Some guys do every weekend or even more often than that. However, I think a fair median is once every other week.

It is also fair to say that most guys that are training go and actually fire live rounds outside of a match on a semi-regular basis. Once a week is fairly frequent for the "average" guy. Some do more and most do less.

One common theme among the people actually training to get better is that they normally spend far more time doing dryfire training than livefire training. It is common for shooters pushing to improve to dryfire five days a week.

I think this above schedule and pattern is very realistic and something that can be stuck with long term. This book is absolutely geared toward people that are looking to do regular training over the long term. Hopefully you can stick with it for a multi-year period of time and experience massive growth in your shooting skills.

The way your training should be organized, if you have a schedule like this, is that you will be doing the vast majority of your repetition and skill building during your dryfire training. A good rule of thumb is that you will pull the trigger dry 10 times for every live round you fire. For many people, this ends up being a very conservative estimate of the volume of dryfire. You don't need to think about it just in terms of pulling the trigger; think about everything. You are going to draw the gun a couple hundred times a day in dryfire and never fire a round. You can do a hundred reloads a night. The list goes on. The point here is that in many respects the dryfire training is going to be your training.

For most people, livefire rounds shot in a match are not going to be very helpful in terms of improving. During a match, you will be concerned with so many things. You will be under pressure to shoot well, and that can be a distraction. Not to mention, you need to interact with your squad and help with scoring/resetting the stage. There is much going on! The match is really the test; it isn't the best way to practice. Not to mention, you only get one run at each stage. There isn't much training value there.

Livefire training is more useful than matches. You will not be distracted by competition and you can shoot each drill as many times as you like. The most effective way to use your livefire training is to test yourself against benchmarks, make sure your gear runs, and observe how things are going. That last part, the *observation* part, is the thing I think people need to do more of. You should be seeing how well you are gripping the gun during your training. Making sure the trigger is pulled straight. You should see how the sights move. You should see if you are over transitioning the gun past targets. During livefire training, you shouldn't be overly "result oriented." There is more happening than just the points you shoot and the time it takes you to shoot them. The key to you improving your score in the future is contained in observing your livefire training very carefully.

For the majority of us, dryfire training is our training. That's it. The technique and habits that you build up in dryfire will carry over to all other aspects of your shooting. If you want to make a technical change to your shooting, work it in to your dryfire training and it will carry over to your livefire and match shooting. You should recognize the fact that practice makes permanent. If you practice holding the gun loosely during dryfire, then that will carry over to your livefire shooting and you won't like the results. You need to be vigilant during your dryfire training to make sure you are doing things properly.

I should also point out that the drills in this book require livefire shooting in order to have the knowledge required to do them well. You need to know what your sights must look like in order to make a shot. You can't learn that without firing ammunition and getting

actual confirmation! Once you know what your sights need to look like at a given distance and difficulty, then you can repeat that in your training, time and time again. This dryfire stuff doesn't just exist in a vacuum. You need to be actually shooting the gun at least a little bit to make sure you are doing things properly.

I have described this phenomenon previously (in other books) as the livefire/dryfire loop. I still think this is the most effective way to explain the process. You figure out what techniques you want to perform, be it how you hold the gun, where you hold it when you reload, or any other detail. You train yourself without using ammunition. You do thousands of repetitions in dryfire. You can then shoot live ammo and see what's what. You then make adjustments to your dryfire training to reflect what you learned in livefire.

To recap these ideas:

1. During the match, just shoot. It is difficult to get training value from a match, especially once you are a seasoned competitor.

2. During your livefire practice, you need to pay attention to more than the points and times. Is the gun staying put in your hands while you shoot? Is your grip consistent? Are the sights moving cleanly from one target to another? Pay attention to the details.

3. Recognize that dryfire training is going to be your training. You will do most of your repetitions without ever using ammunition. This is where you

can make changes to your shooting that will stick with you during the rest of your game.

What to Practice

All the dryfire practice in the world will be of limited value if you aren't practicing the right stuff. It probably isn't a serious concern to the new shooter just getting into the sport. However, after a while you will need to direct your efforts beyond doing what you think is the most fun. Usually, when people hit a plateau, they need to start spending some time figuring out how to approach training in a more systematic fashion.

The whole point of dryfire is to make you a better shooter. I think some people are tempted to get really good at dryfire, just for the sake of being good at it. On the other hand, other people are tempted to restrain themselves from making speed gains in dryfire. They are afraid of being someone that is a dryfire magician that can't actually shoot live ammo properly.

The solution to that conundrum is to monitor your results in livefire. Pay attention to your match results. Above all, be honest with yourself. Make sure you grip your gun "for real." Make sure you are watching your sights for every dryfire shot. The whole point of dryfire is to build habits that make you successful with real bullets. Your results will tell you what is going on.

The key to this whole process is relentless self-analysis. I don't think you need to take it to the point of making yourself crazy or otherwise mentally unstable, but just short of that you need to be constantly evaluating what is happening with your training. Don't let anything slide. Don't wait until some other day to fix a technical problem. Don't settle for sloppy trigger control when you are striving for excellence.

You need to hunt down your weaknesses and relentlessly crush them. If there are technical elements that you find challenging to the point of demoralization, then work through them. If it is hard for you, it is probably hard for everyone else too. You just need to put in the time and you can get better.

Finally, never stop working on the fundamentals. Appropriate sight alignment and appropriate trigger control are an absolute must. If you get sloppy with this, you will seriously damage your shooting. You can do an awful lot of damage in a few thousand incorrect repetitions. Don't be that person.

Ingraining Technique

A large part of the value of dryfire is putting in the repetitions that you permanently ingrain specific techniques by making them subconscious. As a matter of fact, doing dryfire regularly will invariably ingrain your technique. This is a double-edged sword. If you are doing things properly, ingraining those habits are a good thing. If not, then not. A few people I have interacted with have contended that these so called "training scars" are an inevitably side effect of actually training. I can't say I disagree. I think everyone can agree that you want to be doing things as correctly as possible during your dryfire training.

The first step to ingraining the right technique is to make a conscious choice as to the technique you want to use. You need to systematically work out every little detail. Where do you put your hands when you are drawing the gun? Are you using an index point on the frame of the gun when you reload? Are you going to grip the gun high with your non-dominant hand by wrapping fingers up the trigger guard or are you going to stop at the trigger guard? The questions are extensive. If the above questions sound like Greek to you, don't worry. There is enough information on shooting technique alone to fill an entire book (I would know, I wrote one). As your understanding of shooting technique grows, you can make increasingly informed choices about what you are doing. The point is, you need to decide up front how you are going to train yourself.

I want to caution you about letting your body sort it out on its own. For example, it is common advice to just do a lot of draws in order to learn draws. You can certainly do this and in many ways can improve, but you may well train yourself to do counterproductive things. In dryfire, you aren't getting the full experience. You aren't getting the recoil. You aren't dealing with match pressure. You are plenty "warmed up" when you are training. Things may work well during dryfire that don't work with real bullets. The point of dryfire isn't to get good at dryfire. The point is to build habits that make you successful when firing live ammunition. Never lose sight of that perspective.

If you are brand new to the sport, I wouldn't screw around with a timer. Learn to do all the things you need to do. Figure out how to draw. Figure out how to reload. Go through the motions. Emphasize safety. Never sweep yourself. Enforce a 180-degree line in your dryfire area. Check your technique. Get video of yourself and carefully review every little detail. You don't need to be perfect, but look for big technical problems. Are you wildly swinging around when you draw? Are you dropping the gun down when you transition? Fix the big problems, then start working with the timer.

After you become trained to the point where you are smooth and consistent, bring in that time pressure. You will be amazed how fast you can go. The goal times in this manual are entirely reasonable, you just need to make the decision to reach them. It takes many people only a couple weeks to develop an extremely fast draw, but the first step of that process is deciding they are going to chase the goal time.

If you decide that you want to change your technique, then you need to start over. It is almost unavoidable that you at some point will want to change your grip, or change how you stand, or modify some detail of your technique. When you decide to do it, start the whole process over. Take the timer away. Focus on what you are changing. Check out video of yourself. Only then should you bring back in the time pressure.

This is a constant process. Your technique will evolve the longer you stay in the sport, and that is a healthy process. Through diligent work and a desire to improve, you can get anywhere you want to go.

Setting Goals

One of the most important aspects of the drills in this book is the listed goal. I don't think I need to explain in depth that it is an important thing to have goals. It is self-evident that you need to have goals. You need to have that direction. However, if you take a moment and try to come up with what your personal goals are, they are likely not terribly immediate. You want to get better. You want to do well at some match that is six months away. You may want to make GM next year. It is great that you are motivated in all those ways, but I think it is important to focus up on something really specific for the drill that you are working on at that moment.

Instead of going through the motions, so that a year from now you can be "good," I want you to get involved in your practice right now. Try for the listed goal times. Try to nail a specific number of correct repetitions in a row. Try to be noticeably better today than you were yesterday.

The whole point of the goal is to get you invested in your training. If you are unable to achieve the goal, I want you to feel bad about it and work harder. If you are hitting the goals, I want you to feel a sense of achievement and start pushing on the next goal.

The goal times I have specified for each drill are times I believe are appropriate for GM shooters that dryfire with regularity. This isn't to say that if you master these drills in dryfire you will automatically become a GM, but it is to say that you will have a very serious advantage in doing so. If you are already a highly ranked shooter, but you do not dryfire regularly, you will probably find that you can quickly learn to nail the goals that I have specified.

I have a very important message for people that are unable to reach the listed goal times in this book. I think this message will apply to more than 90 percent of the readers:

Don't be discouraged. I have decided to lay down the gauntlet with these goal times. They may well take hundreds of hours of dedicated practice to achieve with regularity. If you are 50 or 70 or even 100 percent slower than the listed goal time, then you should pick a goal for that day that is achievable with some effort on your part. Once you can make your own personal goal time, step yourself up closer to the listed goal time. Any goal time I give you, other than the goal time I have listed, is a goal time that in many respects I just don't believe in. Don't be discouraged by the listed goal times; be motivated by them.

Mistakes

If you are doing dryfire (or livefire for that matter), you are going to make mistakes. In truth, mistakes are something that can't be avoided.

It is commonly said that you need to be perfect with every repetition. I don't believe this to be the case. In the sport of USPSA, you need to be fast. Rushing causes mistakes, but doing everything perfect all the time probably means that you are slow. It probably means you are in your comfort zone. It probably means you aren't advancing your skills very much. Don't be that person.

The fact is, making a mistake here and there doesn't damage your shooting. It doesn't hurt you to screw up sometimes. The practice zone is where you have to work at it to get it right. It is the zone where if you focus, you can nail it. If you try to "phone it in" by getting lazy, you fail.

Try to follow this scheme in your practice:

- If you are pushing so hard that you find yourself unable to get a correct repetition, then you are probably pushing too hard.
- If you screw up occasionally, but generally are able to pull it off, then you are in the zone.
- If you are "perfect," you aren't pushing and thus aren't advancing your skill level.

I do need to offer one caution about mistakes. You need to be aware that you made a mistake in order for it not to count against you. For example, you need to know if you pulled the trigger before you got an appropriate sight picture on a target. If you make mistakes, but are unaware of them, then you are likely to repeat those same mistakes. If you unknowingly repeat your mistakes enough, then those mistakes become habits. Self-awareness is key!

The most important point I can make about mistakes is that you shouldn't fear them. Decide you are going to develop blistering speed, and then do it. You will end up throwing mags across the room when you miss reloads. Your hand will get chewed up from missed draws. Don't worry, everyone who is really fast went through the same thing.

Tension

One issue that I don't feel is adequately understood is that of tension. By "tension," I mean to be addressing muscle tension. Specifically, I want to get right down to your hand tension.

I have four important points I want to make:

1. When you are firing a gun, it is productive to grip the gun pretty hard. Opinions vary on how hard and with which hand and so forth. However, there isn't much disagreement that you should grip the gun pretty hard. I will leave the specifics of that up to your own study.
2. It is much easier to perform the drills in this book with very little tension in your hands and forearms. You move more quickly and precisely when you are relaxed, so this should make good sense to you. This is why people generally like to feel "loose" when they need to move quickly and precisely.
3. When you dryfire, it is very tempting to use a loose grip on the gun. There is no recoil to manage, so there is no immediate incentive to grip the crap out of the gun.

4. When you livefire, the gun bucking in your hand can make you really tense. People sometimes grip the gun so hard they have a hard time letting go of it to shift their grip around to reach the controls.

The point that needs to be made here is that you need to learn variable hand tension. You need to grip the gun really hard when you are pulling the trigger, and only when you are pulling the trigger. At every other time (like when you are reloading), it is much better to be a bit loose.

I recommend you pay attention to this issue during both your livefire and dryfire training, and take steps to correct it if there is a problem. This is problematic with people that rarely livefire, but dryfire frequently. As soon as you develop an awareness of your hand tension you can take steps to correct it.

Remember, it is counter intuitive and difficult to be able to manage your hand tension like this. Your every instinct is going to be to clamp down during livefire and loosen up during dryfire. It is against your human nature to be able to easily master this element of shooting, but with conscious practice it can happen.

Part 4

ELEMENTS

The drills in this section are designed to break fundamental skills apart from each other so you can work on them in isolation from one another. Think about all the things that happen on a regular 30-round long course. There is grip, trigger control, a draw, reloads, target transitions, movements, maybe shooting while moving, and perhaps some other things. Trying to work all of these things into every drill you shoot is unrealistic and inefficient. This section will help you work out each element on its own.

There are some issues that I need to sort through with these drills before you attempt them.

First, I am not going to bog this training manual down with an in-depth discussion of shooting technique. That sort of thing is an entire book on its own. I am going to briefly touch on a few key points. For example, I will discuss grip briefly as it relates to how hard you should hold the gun. However, I just don't have space here to go in-depth on what fingers go precisely where for every hand size and type of gun. *Practical Pistol* has answers to most of those questions already.

Second, some of the drills described here have some extremely tight time limits. We are talking about pushing right to the edge of what you can do with a modern shot timer. Most types of timers have a beep that lasts 0.2 or 0.3 seconds. Further, most timers can only be adjusted in 0.1-second increments. When I specify a par time of 0.4 seconds, you will see those limitations begin to become problematic. For some drills, there may be only a 0.1-second window where you aren't hearing the timer beeping! I have written the goal times in such a way as to account for the nature of dryfire training with a timer, but understand that with time limits this tight, you are going to have to pay special attention to what you are hearing and seeing.

Finally, some of the drills here have no specific time limit at all. I will instead want you to find the edge of your ability and work right on the edge. Please read those instructions very carefully! For example, in the target transitions section, I will ask you to get an appropriate sight picture on a target and then immediately snap to the next target. This means that you can't spend half a second sitting on a target after you get a sight picture on it! You will not feel comfortable transitioning this immediately off a target. That's OK! That's the effect the drill is designed to have! You must be relentlessly honest with yourself about what it is you are seeing and actually accomplishing during these drills in order for them to have the desired effect. If you don't work, the drill won't work.

Slow Fire Trigger Control

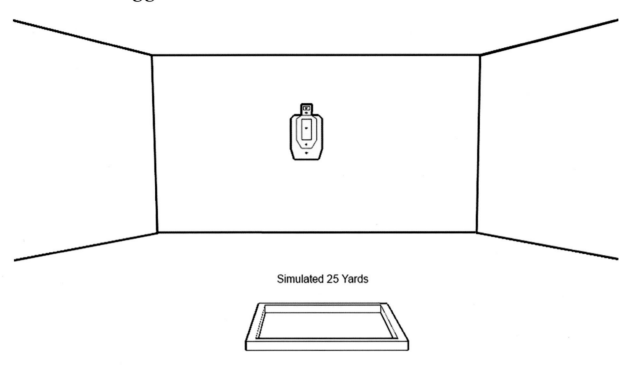

Simulated 25 Yards

Date:	Notes:

Setup Notes:
This drill only requires a single target.

Procedure:
Aim your pistol at the target. Align the sights as well as you can, then press the trigger without disturbing that alignment. There is *no time limit* for this drill.

Alternate freestyle shooting and single-handed shooting. Be sure to use both trigger modes if you are using a DA/SA trigger.

Focus:
Perfect your ability to shoot accurately with no time limit. You should build an awareness of proper grip and trigger finger placement.

Goal:

Keep the sights perfectly still as you push the trigger straight back. You shouldn't perceive any movement in the sights at all.

Commentary:

Slowly drawing your pistol from the holster, gripping it properly, and then carefully breaking the shot so as not to disturb the sight alignment is what many noncompetitive shooters think of as dryfire. This drill is it for them. As competitive shooters, we can do so much more. However, we still need to be able to do this drill.

I really like to focus on the sensation of moving your trigger finger in isolation. So many people have an ingrained habit where they pull the trigger using muscles from their whole hand. By doing a bit of dryfire, these people can get a sense of what it feels like to fire an accurate shot. Watching the sights will tell you the whole story about what your hand is actually doing. If you see the sights wiggle when you are pressing the trigger, you are doing it wrong.

It usually doesn't take many repetitions for someone to start doing this with minimal problems. There are many shooters that can perform good trigger control in dryfire, but they can't do it at the range. If you are in this category, you should recognize that *any* disruption of your sight picture when you press the trigger back will absolutely show up downrange.

You should make sure that you hold the gun as hard as you would when you shoot live ammunition. This means hold it as hard as you can with your nondominant hand. You need to keep your firing hand loose enough so you can actually move your trigger finger in isolation. Focus on this feeling!

You should also pay attention to trigger finger placement on the face of the trigger. This should help you feel the way you are pressing the trigger back into the frame of the gun. Is the trigger going straight back? Do you need to adjust your finger/hand position? Typically, shooters get a better result by grabbing a bit more trigger and getting more leverage. Use this drill to check yourself and make sure you are putting the pressure straight back.

I recommend that you master this drill in dryfire. When you are out on the range trying to perfect your slow fire trigger control and using real ammo, don't hesitate to unload your gun and reacquaint yourself with this drill. Alternating between livefire and dryfire will help you isolate the right "feel" in your hands and trigger finger.

Trigger Control at Speed

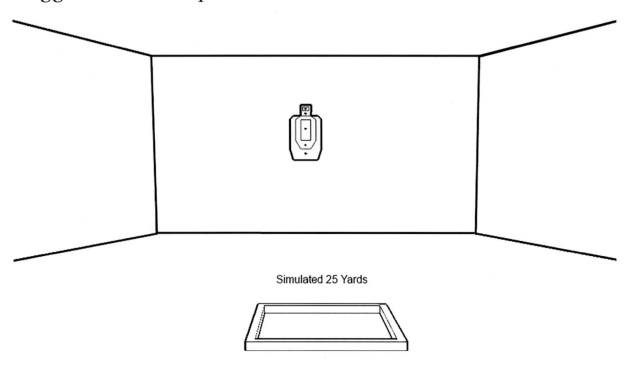

Simulated 25 Yards

Date:	Notes:

Setup Notes:
This drill only requires a single target.

Procedure:
Set your timer for a "random" start.

Aim your pistol at the target. Align the sights as well as you can. At the signal, press the trigger quickly. A good rule of thumb for "quickly" is that you should be done pressing the trigger at the end of the start signal. DO NOT "prep" your trigger for this drill. All the trigger pressing must be done after the start signal.

Alternate freestyle shooting and single-handed shooting. Be sure to use both trigger modes if you are using a DA/SA trigger. For double-action trigger mode, it is acceptable to press the trigger a bit less aggressively than single action mode.

Focus:

Perfect your ability to shoot accurately with a time limit.

Goal:

The goal here is to be able to press your trigger fast and straight. This drill will reveal trigger control faults to you, and you will be able to correct them. Pressing the trigger fast and straight should become absolutely second nature.

Commentary:

This drill is designed to make you strive for a perfect trigger press while under severe time restraints. This will help with learning to hit long shots under match pressure, as well as helping you refine your grip.

I want to draw your attention to a few things in the procedure to make sure they are clearly understood. This drill stipulates that you press the trigger quickly when you hear the start beep. "Quickly" is designed to be your realistic match pace. Most shooters yank the trigger back very quickly when they are at a match. They also miss a lot. I don't want you to slow down for this drill; I want you to learn to press the trigger straight.

The really important element in the procedure is learning to break the trigger without disturbing what sight picture you do have. That is really the tricky part. The important thing to bring to this drill from your livefire training is to understand that the trigger control is by far the most important element in accuracy. You can make long shots, even with misaligned sights, provided that you execute proper trigger control. If you understand that point, this drill will make much more sense to you.

Draw

Simulated 7 Yards

Date:	Notes:

Setup Notes:
This drill only requires a single target.

Procedure:
Start with your hands relaxed at sides. At the signal, draw your pistol and aim it at the target. Do not pull the trigger.

Focus:
Learn to draw quickly and consistently.

Goal:
Draw your pistol and get a sight picture with a *good* grip in 0.7 seconds, 0.6 seconds if you are using a "speed" holster.

You may alternate start positions if you wish. Add 0.1 second to start with your wrists above your shoulders. Add 0.2 seconds if you start facing directly uprange. Add 0.2 seconds if you use the head box as your target.

Commentary:

Your draw is an important element to master. You might think the draw doesn't matter that much because you do relatively few draws in a match compared to all the other rounds you fire. However, I have found that draw speed and consistency are strongly correlated with speed on all sorts of stages. When you draw, you look to a spot on a target and put the sights on that spot as quickly as you can. This is the same concept as a normal target transition.

Your draw is where your grip and sight alignment converge to create something many people call an "index." You need that index, so you can look to a spot and have the sights show up in alignment on that spot quickly and consistently.

When you draw your gun, there are a few sensations you need to pay careful attention to. Most importantly, when the gun comes up onto the target you want a "crush" grip on the gun. Your nondominant hand should be giving 100 percent of available grip strength and should be positioned properly on the gun. This needs to be done as soon as the gun hits your eyeline so you can fire when you see the sights where you want them. There shouldn't be any time spent cleaning up your grip when the gun is already up. That needs to be done on the way up to your eyes.

In terms of sight picture, you want to see the sights (or the dot) come up and settle into the center of the target. You don't want to see the sight come down onto the target from above. This means the gun went over the target and came down. It is a bit of a waste of energy to bring the gun up only to bring it down again.

The sight picture shouldn't bounce around wildly when the gun gets to the target. This is indicative of you "throwing" the gun up and not bringing it up in a controlled fashion. The idea is to get the gun into a position where you can realistically shoot it. Being out of control does you no good.

One very important thing to point out here is that you shouldn't pull the trigger on this drill. I don't want you put in a situation where you are racing the stop beep with the click from the trigger pull. That isn't really the point here. Also, we are just working on one element at a time! Do yourself a favor and don't pull the trigger during this training. Pay attention to your grip and your sight pictures instead.

I have also attached some "micro" drills. You absolutely should do them! These drills break the draw process down in to a couple distinct pieces and should help you nail down the areas where you are having problems.

I also listed a couple variations in terms of start position or using the head box as a target. Use those variations to make sure you are prepared for the common start positions you will see in the sport.

Micro Drills:

Drill One:

Start with your hands relaxed at sides. Get a firing grip on your pistol and move your nondominant hand over to your dominant side.

Your goal is a 0.4-second par time, with time to spare.

Drill Two:

Start with your gun holstered. Have a firing grip on your pistol with your dominant hand and have your nondominant hand in position to receive the gun after you draw it. From this start position, draw and aim at the target.

Your goal is a 0.5-second par time.

Optional Drill:

Attach your timer to your holster. From a wrists above shoulders start position, slap the timer when you hear the start signal. The timer should pick up that slap and record a time. Strive to make that time as low as possible.

Reload

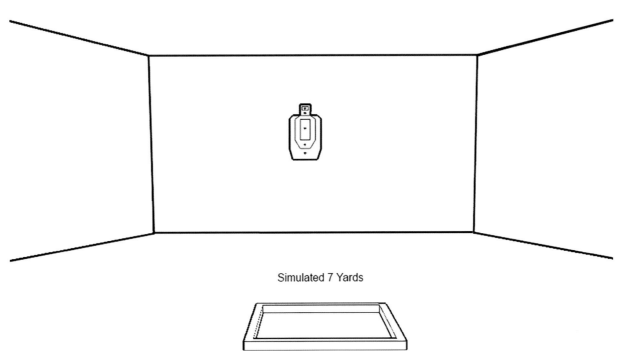

Simulated 7 Yards

Date:	Notes:

Setup Notes:
This drill only requires a single target.

Procedure:
Start with your pistol aimed at the target. At the signal, eject the magazine from the gun and insert a new magazine. Get another sight picture on the target. Do not pull the trigger.

Focus:
Learn to reload quickly and consistently.

Goal:
Your goal is a 1.0-second par time.

Commentary:

Reloading is a skill that many people find to be much tougher than drawing. That makes sense, as there is a much more complicated series of actions to learn to perform under pressure. Technical issues, such as how to position the gun when you reload, are things that must be sorted out by the individual. Generally speaking, you will be more consistent if you bring the gun lower down and closer to your body. I strongly recommend you pay close attention to how you angle the magwell of your pistol. I make sure to angle my gun so the magwell points at my mag pouches. Figure out what works for you, then train yourself to use that technique every time.

The biggest challenge I have during these drills is the urge to tense up. When you are tense, it is almost impossible to quickly and consistently hit your reloads. I think that is a great challenge that should prepare you for competition. If you can learn to battle that tension (and occasional frustration) in a dryfire setting, then your odds of success "for real" get that much better. Make sure you start holding the gun with a firm and realistic firing grip, reload, then finish back on a realistic firing grip.

There are a couple other issues that bear mentioning here. Be sure you prepare yourself for common circumstances. You need to be prepared to drop an empty magazine from the gun as well as a full one. You need to be able to quickly actuate the slide stop, if the slide is open. Don't only practice slide forward reloads with full magazines. Be ready

for anything. Of course, you will lose a bit of time on most guns if you need to rack the gun, but you should be prepared to reload an entirely empty gun. It does happen in competition, and you want to minimize the damage to your score. The bottom line here is that you should be ready to do an efficient reload in all circumstances.

I have a couple administrative notes regarding the below micro drills.

First, it is obviously much more expedient to run Drill One, then Drill Two, then Drill One again. The start position of Drill Two is the same as the ending position of Drill One. This should save you from constantly having to reset your magazines in the pouch.

Second, the goal times are set for your first magazine pouch. I encourage you to work through all of your magazine pouches in dryfire practice, but you should understand that when you start reaching around your body for your fourth magazine pouch, you will likely be quite a bit slower. I have heard the assertion, on a few occasions, that you should be equally fast from all magazine pouches, but I have never observed this to be the case with my own shooting and I do not have that expectation of anyone else.

Micro Drills:
Drill One:

(**Burkett Load**) Start with your pistol aimed at the target. At the signal, eject the magazine from the gun and bring the fresh magazine just to the edge of the magwell. You can do this drill without ejecting a magazine if you wish, just be sure that you press the magazine release button hard enough to actually function.

Your goal is a 0.6-second par time.

Drill Two:

Start with a magazine in your hand, just at the edge of the magwell of your pistol. This start position should be exactly the same as the ending position of Drill One.

At the signal, seat the magazine, reacquire your grip, and get a sight picture on the target.

Your goal is a 0.6-second par time.

Target Transitions

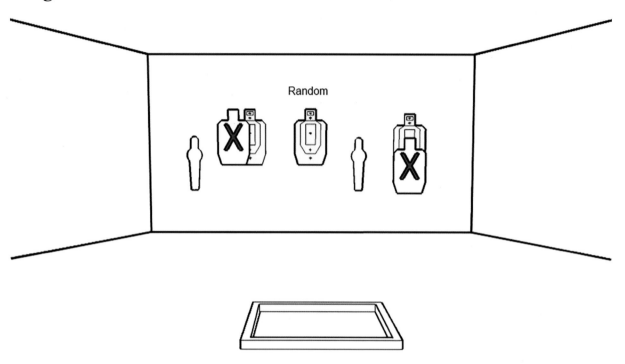

Date:	Notes:

Setup Notes:

The targets should be set up in a random fashion. It is NOT necessary or even desirable to have the targets set up the same way every time. Change things up! Be sure to vary the target spacing, distance, and difficulty.

Procedure:

Start with your hands relaxed at sides, facing downrange. At the signal, draw and get a sight picture on each target. The sight picture should be appropriate, given the simulated distance and difficulty of the target. The instant you get a sight picture on that target, go to the next target. Set a par time and work to lower it over the course of your training session. Do not touch the trigger during this drill or attempt to simulate actually shooting the targets in any way. Get sight pictures only!

Focus:

Develop the ability to look at a spot and drive the gun to that spot.

Goal:

Your goal is to gain the ability to look at a spot and have the gun "cleanly" go to that spot. You should observe and correct common mistakes, such as pushing the gun too far, stopping the gun too early, and aiming in the wrong spot.

Commentary:

Learning to transition the gun around aggressively is one of those things that will make a huge difference in your stage times. Speed from one target to the next is something that holds back many mid-level shooters.

This drill requires that you get a proper sight picture on one target, then the next, and then the next. Obviously, the focus is on speeding up that process. The one thing you can't get from dryfire here is to know what your sights need to look like on a given target distance/difficulty. Is it OK to just have target focus or do you need a sharp sight focus? How much sight misalignment is acceptable?

You get the answers to these questions during your livefire training. You can then bring that knowledge to your dryfire. In general, it is fair to say that you can get away with much more than you think! No matter what you decide regarding sight pictures, you need to *consciously* decide before you start training.

When doing this drill, be sure you get your sight picture on the targets and then immediately move to the next one. Do not stare at a "good" sight picture on the target confirming what you already know. The instant the sights look good, you should be looking to the next target. The goal here is to shoot with that same level of immediacy. In addition to building speed, you should be looking to shift attention from one target to the next with no delay. You are going to train yourself to work faster than conscious thought.

In terms of technique, it is critical that you keep most of your body loose. You only hold the gun with your hands! Adding in muscle tension in your abs, your back, or your shoulders is not productive. That additional tension makes it difficult to stop the gun in the center of any given target, if you are aggressively transitioning the gun to that target. Watch out for over transitioning. This occurs when you put too much muscle into the gun and swing it past your intended target. If you see the sights go past your target and then travel back to your aim point, it is an indication that you are too tense.

Regarding the par time setting, you are looking to push that down until you find your limit. You should see the sights smoothly settling in the center of each target and then immediately moving to the next target. If that is happening, then set a faster par time. That having been said, keep in mind the only purpose here is to work on the transitions. If you are screwing up your draw/grip in the pursuit of speed, then you can switch to starting with the gun already in your hands. That isn't an issue.

Movement

Date:	Notes:

Setup Notes:

This drill requires two shooting positions. Designate two shooting positions and mark them on the ground some way. Make these positions about five yards apart. You must also designate which targets you shoot from which position. You can move in any direction (forward, backward, laterally), but it is easiest to master lateral movement first.

Procedure:

Start with your hands relaxed at sides, facing downrange. At the signal, draw and get a sight picture on each target you are to engage from that position. Move to the second position and repeat. Establish a par time and work to reduce it.

Focus:

Work to move immediately and quickly from one shooting position to another. Work on being ready when arriving at the next shooting position.

Goal:

The goal here is to be able to operate at the limits of your body. You should move absolutely as aggressively as you can from one spot to the next, have the gun up and ready to go when you get in to a new shooting position, and have the ability to stabilize yourself with your legs as you set up in a shooting position.

Commentary:

The first thing I want to do in this commentary is explain the goal a bit more in detail. The goal here isn't a specific time; it is more a feeling. If you move as aggressively as you can, then that's all anyone can ask. That may seem obvious, but the fact is most lower level shooters do not move through the stage at their maximum aggression level, far from it. When I push students to move faster and more explosively, they usually start losing their balance and sliding around on the range. This is due to being inexperienced at moving explosively, not a lack of muscle power. If you actually move at 100 percent of your capacity, you will learn to control your body and get yourself stabilized as you come into a position. If there isn't a feeling, at least initially, that you are "out of control" with your movements, you probably are not going at a true 100 percent.

In terms of technique, there are a couple of major issues here.

First, you need to get into a stable stance as you move around. Get your legs set up wide and get your weight down a little bit lower. This will give you stability as you enter and exit your shooting positions. You should have a sensation of your body weight stopping dead in your tracks as you get into a shooting position. If you don't have that, you need to reassess what's going on with your technique.

When you move into a shooting position, the gun should be up high where you can see the sights. A couple steps or so before you are stopped, you should already be aiming at the first target you intend to shoot in the position you are getting into. The idea is that you want to prepare yourself to start shooting as soon as the sights tell you that you will get good center hits on the target.

As you work through this drill, be sure you carefully watch your sights! They are going to tell you the whole story about your stability level as you move around. If you see your sights bouncing as you come into a new shooting position, you need to fix that with your legs and knees in order to get stable. You don't want to wait too long to be shooting or slow down your movement in order to gain stability. The goal here is to be aggressive *and* stable. Don't give up until you achieve that.

Shooting While Moving

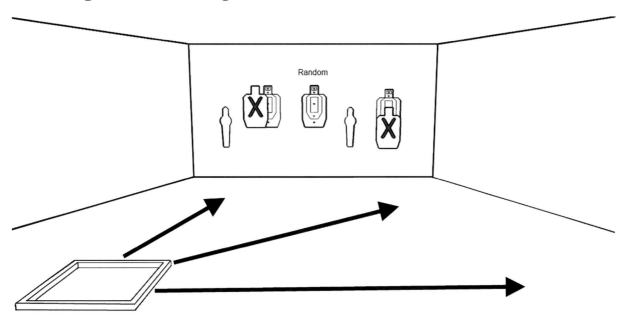

Date:	Notes:

Procedure:

Start with your hands relaxed at sides, facing downrange. At the signal, draw and get a sight picture on each target as you move in the direction of your choosing. Establish a par time and work to both increase the distance you can move in that time while maintaining accuracy and reduce the time itself.

Focus:

Develop the ability to look at a spot and drive the gun to that spot while you are moving. Work to develop stability in your sight picture.

Goal:

You should be able to move quickly and maintain a stable sight picture. You also should have a clear idea of your limitations in terms of how quickly you can move and hit targets.

Commentary:

Shooting while your feet are moving is a key skill to master in order to be able to effectively get into and out of shooting positions. I strongly recommend that you try this drill in livefire before you get too deep into your dryfire training. You need to have a good sense of how stable your sights need to be in order to fire accurate shots. Many people are in the habit of letting their sights bounce all over the place, and if you do that you will have a hard time getting "A" zone hits. Learn what the sights need to look like in livefire first, then go home and practice making that happen. A good rule of thumb here is to take whatever sight picture you like on a static target and then add 50 percent to the distance if you plan to shoot the target moving. For example, I aim at a 10-yard target I plan to shoot while moving as if it is a 15-yard static target.

Another dryfire-specific issue for this sort of training is to point out that target scaling makes a big difference here. If you aren't moving then the target scale isn't a big deal, but if you start moving around then a 1/3 scale target gets bigger or smaller really quick! If possible, you should try this drill at a range, so you can more easily use full-size targets (due to how much space is required). Half-scale targets are easily acquired and are a good compromise for this drill. I wouldn't recommend doing this drill on anything smaller than 1/3-scale target.

One thing that bears discussion is the procedure for this drill. Your goal is to both move further as you shoot (indicating that you can cover more ground on a stage) and shoot faster (reducing the par time). You can alternate your focus on these things. You never know what a stage will bring you. There may be relatively large distances to cover with only a couple close ranged targets. In this scenario, you would want to engage those targets at as close to a flat-out run as possible. In other situations, you may have small distances to cover with lots of targets where you can more trot through the stage shooting the whole time. Be ready for anything!

Micro Drill:

Start with your pistol at low ready (in a comfortable two-handed grip, pointed at a 45-degree angle toward the floor). At the signal, point the pistol at a target and get a sight picture. Do not pull the trigger. As soon as you hear the start signal, you are required to move. You may move in any direction desired. Alternate movement direction.

Your goal is a 0.5-second par time.

One-Handed Shooting

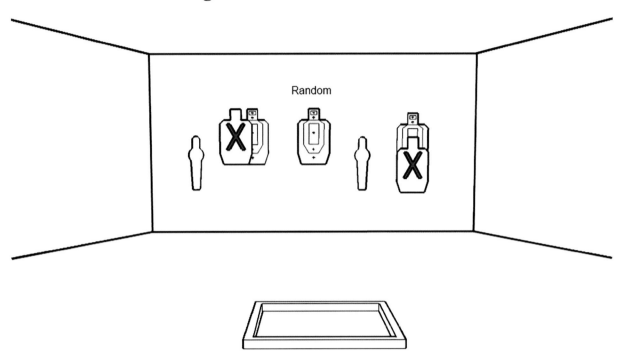

Date:	Notes:

Procedure:

Start with your hands relaxed at sides, facing downrange. At the signal, draw and engage each target with the appropriate number of rounds while using only one hand. Do two shots for paper targets and one shot if you are simulating steel targets. You will be working both strong hand only and weak hand only for this drill. Establish a separate par time for each and work to reduce them.

Focus:

Develop a comfortable and consistent single-handed shooting technique.

Goal:

You should have a developed "index" for strong hand only and weak hand –only shooting. You need to be able to look to a spot and have the sights line up on that spot. You should be confident in your ability to shoot only one handed.

Commentary:

Shooting with only one hand is something that you will occasionally need to do in competition. The mechanics are different enough to freestyle shooting that it warrants a bit of discussion in this section.

First, I think you should make a point to grip the gun as hard as you can when shooting with only one hand. That is a big part of my dryfire focus. The gun needs to be locked into my hand as rock solid as I can get it. If I am gripping it 100 percent as hard as I can, it shouldn't fly around a whole lot when shooting live ammunition. It doesn't matter if it is strong hand only or weak hand only, I am going to grip as hard as possible.

Another thing you should make a point of doing is working on your trigger control. Press the trigger back into the frame *hard and fast*.

Make sure you don't see the sights moving around. When you actually shoot live ammo, you are probably going to press forward in to the recoil and try to keep the gun from recoiling up. Prepare yourself for that sensation by pressing hard during dryfire so you can see if you will be pushing shots down into the bottom of the target. That is something you want to fix in dryfire before it bites you during livefire.

Another thing that needs to be discussed here is having a safe transfer to your weak hand when shooting only weak-handed. You will draw the gun with your strong hand and move it up to your eyeline and do the transfer there. The technical specifics don't matter a whole lot. Some people grab the gun differently when they are going to transfer it. That doesn't matter a whole lot. What does matter is that you look at the gun during the transfer to make sure you are doing it properly. Don't bother watching the targets until you get a weak-handed grip on the gun.

Finally, you will need to work with a par time for each hand. The transfer to your weak hand will add quite a bit to your time, so it isn't realistic to expect to be the same speed weak-handed as you are strong-handed.

Part 5
STANDARDS

"Standards" are known distance and time drills where you can get up to a competitive speed with the rest of the field. The other drills in this book are largely left up to you to set the par times. These drills aren't. Shooters all over the world use these same drills and times to train, so obviously, they do a good job as a group of setting the bar in an appropriate place.

These times are going to be challenging for most shooters. They may well feel impossible. That's not a bad thing, it just means you have a lot of work to do. I recommend you revisit the "elements" training if you are having problems in this section. Those isolation exercises are going to help you immeasurably in this section. You need to develop the high-speed draws, reloads, index, and the ability to transition at the speed of your eyes. Without those tools in place, these standards will be an uphill battle.

If you are plateaued in your training and need to get faster, then these drills should become an area of particular focus. You may have to push to get to the next level, but with some effort you can make it happen. Many shooters are afraid to make mistakes in their dryfire training. They think that will invariably cause mistakes at matches. I think otherwise. It is entirely OK to make mistakes during your training so long as you have discipline to perform what you can at a consistent speed whenever you decide to do that. With those fundamentals in place, there is nothing wrong with pushing to the point of failure. I can assure you that the top shooters in the world pushed themselves to get where they are. Magazines get thrown across the room. Guns are dropped. Things happen. You shouldn't make potentially dangerous mistakes with live ammunition involved, but dryfire practice at home is a different story.

I also should call your attention to the setup of these drills. Most of them are done on a single target or an "El Prez Array." You can and should set up some targets in this fashion and just leave them set up. Unlike the scenarios elsewhere in the book where change is good, change isn't so good on these drills. These are supposed to be standards! Set up your targets and leave them set. There isn't a specified spacing between that targets delineated on the diagrams in this section. Due to the way targets get scaled it just isn't practical to insist on that level of detail in your setup. Just set the targets so they have a couple targets worth of space between them and you should be fine.

I also have included a few drills that require a bit of movement. I wanted to give you some specific tests for your movement skills and some specific times to shoot for. I think your actual movement training and skill building should be done on a broader scope of drills, but I think it is very helpful to at least give the reader an idea of what should happen.

Bill Drill

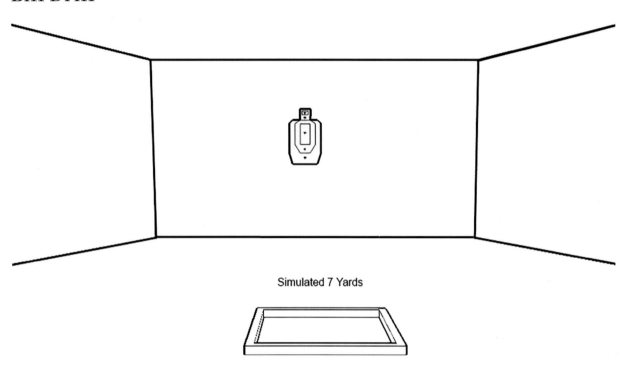

Simulated 7 Yards

Date:	Notes:

Procedure:

Start with your hands relaxed at sides or wrists above shoulders. Engage the target with six shots.

Focus:

Develop your draw, trigger, and grip mechanics.

Goal:

A par time of 1.6 seconds is reasonable.

Commentary:

I view the Bill Drill more a test of a good draw, rather than anything else. You draw into your grip and obviously shoot while using that grip. I don't think it is particularly challenging to nail down a fast time on this drill, what is challenging is doing it while you are gripping the gun properly. *I recommend you pay close attention to your hand tension.* You will probably find that it is much easier to produce a fast time while you are loose, but you are doing yourself a disservice longer term.

I think what shooters need to learn is the ability to hold the gun *very* firm, but move the trigger finger independently of that. When you actually start firing real bullets, it may well cause your whole body to tense up. With some dryfire training, where you pay attention to managing your hand pressure, I think you can set yourself up to counteract much of your natural tendency to tense up.

Another thing that is absolutely critical to pay attention to is how hard you are physically pressing the trigger. Many people have a hard time learning to run the trigger quickly under recoil. They get too tense in their firing hand and the muscles don't respond properly. This leads to trigger freeze. It happens even more frequently when the shooter is making a deliberate attempt to "go fast." The best dryfire method I have found to overcome this is to deliberately press the trigger really hard during dryfire. Take how hard you think you need to press during livefire and double it for dryfire. This introduces a lot of tension into your firing hand and helps you work through the problem rather than only experience it when shooting real bullets.

Once again, the point of this drill is for you to train your muscles to have the appropriate levels of tension and to put the right amount of force into the gun. With enough training (both livefire and dryfire), you will be able to control the gun subconsciously and run the trigger very quickly when the situation calls for it.

4 Aces

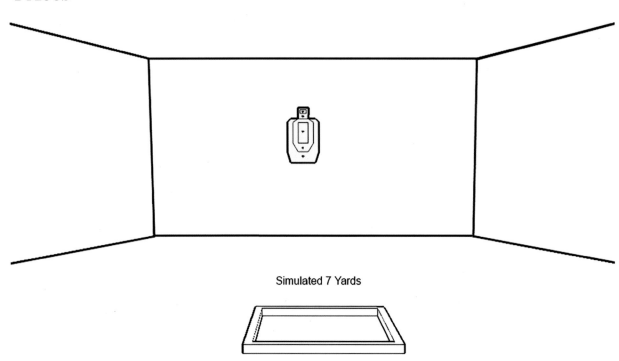

Simulated 7 Yards

Date:	Notes:

Procedure:

Start with your hands relaxed at sides or wrists above shoulders. Engage the target with two shots. Reload and reengage with two more shots.

Focus:

Develop your draw, reload, and trigger speed.

Goal:

A par time of 1.8 seconds is reasonable.

Commentary:

Four Aces is a very challenging standard to meet. This requires both drawing and reloading in under a second. The complication is further added by spending little time actually on target. It makes the shooter feel very "busy" during the drill. It is tough to get it right, that's for sure. The whole point here is to build solid mechanics so you can nail down fast standing reloads when you are forced to do one in a match.

One thing that is very critical here is learning how to position your gun for the reload. For guns that don't have a magwell, most shooters are going to want to drop the gun down a bit and angle it more toward the magazine pouches. I find that angle to be absolutely critical to a good performance. If the magwell of the gun is pointed away from my chest at a 90-degree angle, then it is much tougher than getting the magwell directed toward the pouches (more like a 45-degree angle). Of course, every shooter and gun setup is a bit different. You should pay attention to the angles on this drill and get things set up to work for you.

Another thing that can be a problem is building up excess tension during this drill. You need to hold the gun hard to shoot effectively, but at the speed you will be drawing and reloading, if that tension makes its way down into your arms it will almost certainly cause missed reloads and slow times. Focus only on holding the gun with your hands and keeping your arms and upper body a bit looser.

El Prez

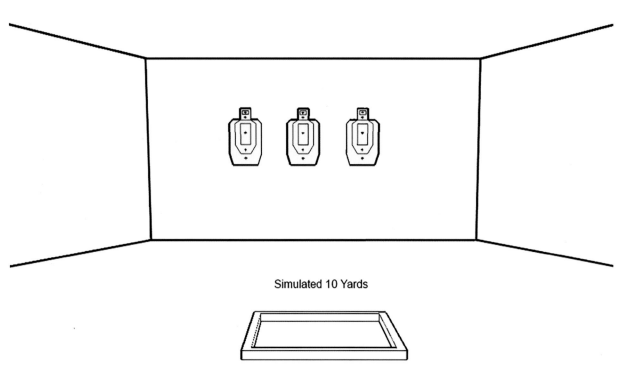

Simulated 10 Yards

Date:	Notes:

Procedure:

Start with your wrists above shoulders, facing uprange. At the signal, turn, draw, and engage each target with two rounds. Reload and reengage each target with an additional two rounds.

Focus:

Put together drawing, transitioning, and reloading into one classic test.

Goal:

Your goal is a 4.0-second par time.

Commentary:

The "El Prez" stands alone as a good drill, *the* standard test, and an iconic training exercise. Very few shooters that have been around for a while have not shot this at one time or another.

I view this as a good aggregate test of a bunch of fundamental skills. You need to nail the draw, reload, transitions, and you battle a bit of instability from turning around.

The goal time of 4.0 seconds is very achievable if you are able to nail all of the preceding drills, there is no doubt about that. With that in mind, the key is figuring out where you are deficient, if you are unable to hit the 4.0 second par time. Perhaps your draw is a bit slow. Maybe you can't reload fast enough. I encourage you to take a step back and figure out specifically what you need to do. Again, this should be obvious if you are actually working through the previously mentioned drills in this book.

Resist the temptation to just "go faster" in order to hit the par time. When the drills get longer and more complicated like this one, people have a real tendency to go crazy in order to hit the goal time. Be very honest with yourself about what your sight picture looks like and how your grip feels. Make sure you get that stuff down. If you are having problems, go and work on those specific problems individually, then come back and try this drill again.

I think the only challenge that you find in the "El Prez," that you don't necessarily see in every other drill, is the turning draw. This should only add a couple tenths of a second to your draw time. I prefer to turn into a squared up and comfortable stance. Other people prefer to simply turn and get on target as fast as they possibly can. No matter what you decide, the turn doesn't need to add much time. Just snap your head onto the first target and drive the gun to it.

Distance Draw

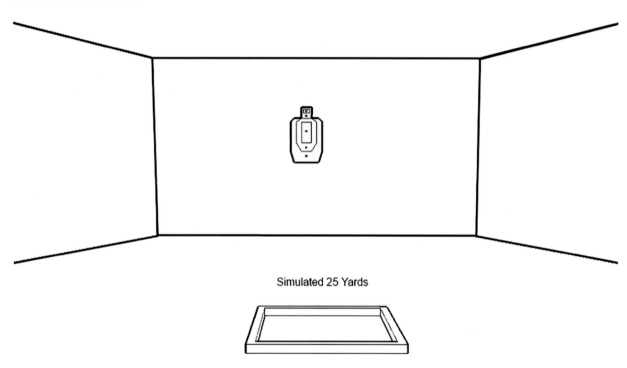

Simulated 25 Yards

Date:	Notes:

Procedure:

Start with your hands relaxed at sides. At the signal, draw your pistol and acquire a sight picture on the target. The sight picture should be appropriate in order to get you an "A" zone hit at your simulated 25-yard distance. *Do not* pull the trigger for this drill.

Focus:

Refine your draw to the point where you can draw down on long targets with confidence and precision.

Goal:

A 1.0-second par time to draw to a sight picture is your goal for this drill.

Commentary:

The "Distance Draw" isn't *fundamentally* different from drawing on a closer ranged target, but you will need to focus on a couple different things than you otherwise might if you are working closer in.

First, I want to call your attention to the goal. Your goal is getting a sight picture in the specified time. That sight picture must be appropriate to the target, meaning you need the sights to be aligned very well and stable enough to actually make that 25-yard shot. This isn't as easy as it sounds. For me personally, I don't "slam" the gun into position on difficult targets. I let the sights settle into the target much more gently. This doesn't mean you draw more slowly, on the contrary, you will not have time to waste by slowing down your draw. You just need to finish the draw much more gently. Try to get a sensation of the sights coming up and settling into the center of the target, rather than having them wobble around a lot when they get up to your eyeline.

Next, pay very close attention to the quality of your grip on this drill. You will find that if things are even microscopically out of position, you will bring the sights up on target and have them not be in alignment. Of course, the solution to that problem in a match setting is to fix your sight alignment and then shoot, but for the purposes of this drill you will fail to meet the par time. Keep working on your grip so your sights show up on target just about perfectly every time.

I feel this drill gets neglected by shooters that are chasing faster times on the closer ranged drills. Don't make that mistake. You need to get conversant with what is required to get your sights aligned quickly on longer ranged targets. This will pay dividends even if a long target isn't your first target of a stage.

Distance One-Handed Draw

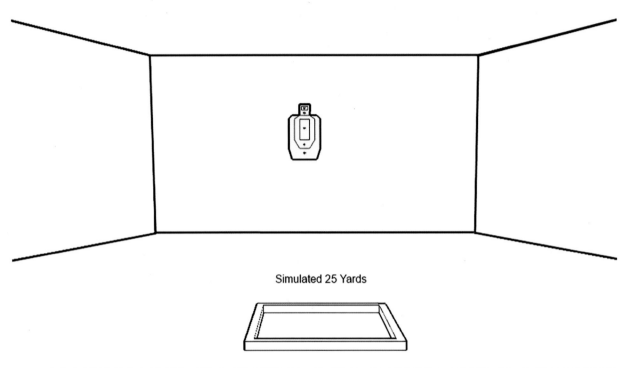

Simulated 25 Yards

Date:	Notes:

Procedure:
Start with your hands relaxed at sides or wrists above shoulders. At the signal, draw your pistol and get a sight picture on the target. *Do not* pull the trigger for this drill.

Focus:
Develop the ability to draw onto a distant target with one hand.

Goal:
Strong hand only, your par time is 1.2 seconds.

Weak hand only, your par time is 1.8 seconds.

Commentary:
The time limits on this drill are tight as ever, but certainly makeable.

I think it is fair to say that even some very good shooters will struggle with getting on target with the level of precision that this drill demands. Simply put, we just don't see much 25-yard shooting with one hand only. That doesn't mean this isn't a valid exercise. I think being able to grip your pistol perfectly enough to get right on your sights on a difficult target will put you in good stead to make any one-handed shot required of you in competition. Not to mention the confidence you will feel when you step up to the line and engage "normal" distance targets with one hand.

When you are doing this drill weak-handed, obviously much of the key is in the transfer. If anything, I take my time on the transfer to make sure I get my grip as close to perfect as possible, then I get out on target. If you miss your grip, you may well be hunting for your front sight (or your dot) when you hear the second beep.

The final point to emphasize here is that you should make a point of getting a "crush" grip on the gun. Since you will be shooting one handing gripping as hard as you can you should work that in to your training. Grip down hard when the gun is getting on target.

Long Distance Draw

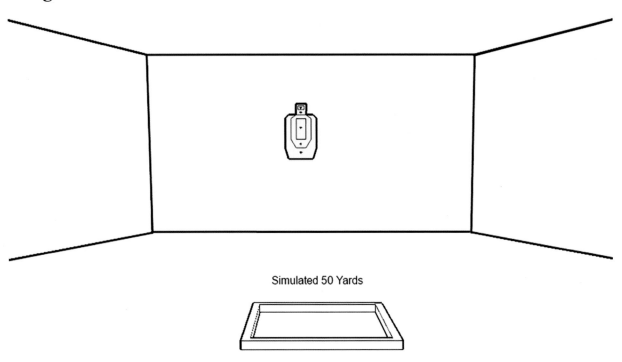

Simulated 50 Yards

Date:	Notes:

Procedure:

Start with your hands relaxed at sides. At the signal, draw your pistol and acquire a sight picture on the target. The sight picture must be "equal height, equal light," in order to get you an "A" zone hit at your simulated 50-yard distance. **Do not** pull the trigger for this drill.

Focus:

The focus here is to draw your pistol to a stable and refined sight picture. This is less about pure speed and more about accuracy.

Goal:

Your goal is a 1.3-second par time.

Commentary:

The point of this drill is to develop the ability to get to an absolutely perfect sight picture as soon as you possibly can. Perfect is not an understatement here. Your sights must be for all intents and purposes *perfect* in order to get center hits at the 50-yard line.

I think it is counterproductive to slow your draw stroke down for tougher targets, at least until you get the gun close to being on target.

It does make sense to let the gun settle into the target as opposed to jamming it into position. When I see the sights gently settle into the "A" box, I know I am doing this drill correctly.

Obviously, you are going to need to get an appropriately scaled target in order to simulate 50 yards of distance. I wouldn't worry about having perforations on the target. You probably can't see them when you are shooting at 50 yards anyway.

Partials

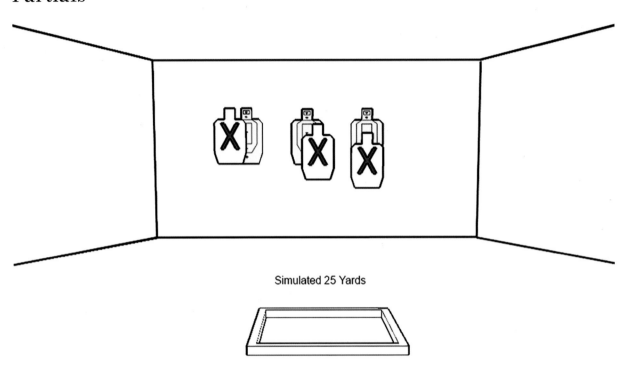

Simulated 25 Yards

Date:	Notes:

Setup Notes:
Three half "A" zone partials at 25 yards (leave half the "A" zone, however you want to do it).

Procedure:
Engage each target with two rounds. Alternate among common starting positions.

Focus:
The goal here is to refine marksmanship fundamentals.

Goal:
Your goal is a 3.5-second par time.

Commentary:

This drill will push your fundamentals to the limit. The targets should be simulating the most difficult shots in the sport. The time limit is borderline insane. Under these circumstances, you can't help but get better.

Pay careful attention to the aiming points you select on the targets. You should have a good idea (based on your livefire training) of where exactly your pistol hits at any given range, and you want to train yourself to put the sights exactly where they need to go. So frequently, people have a habit of holding too high or holding too low, and it is a very difficult habit to break. It may not make a big difference for the majority of shots in the sport, but I can assure you that at 25 yards you will know if you are holding the gun in the wrong spot on the targets.

I wouldn't insist entirely on perfection when you work this drill. In many ways, it is OK if you can spot the "bad ones" and know where your misaligned shots are going. This will help you hop on the learning curve longer term.

Triple Reloads

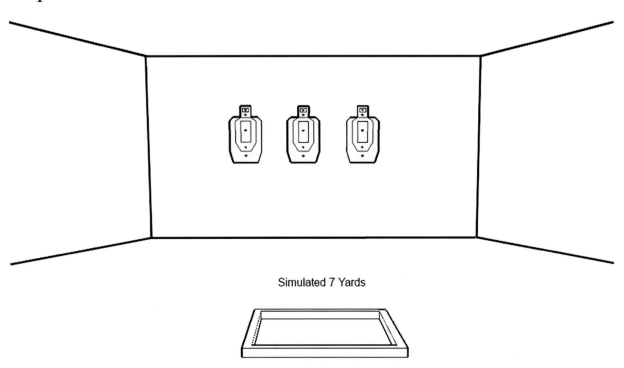

Simulated 7 Yards

Date:	Notes:

Procedure:

Start with your hands relaxed at sides or wrists above shoulders.

Engage one target with six rounds, reload, and engage another target with six rounds, reload, and engage the final target with six rounds.

Focus:

Work on reloading your pistol.

Goal:

Your goal is a 4.8-second par time.

Commentary:

Often when doing dryfire drills, the challenge is to fire one or two shots and then hit a reload, then fire one or two shots, then reload, etc. This drill is a more "practical" test of your reloading skills. You will fire six rounds in between reloads, letting you get into a firing rhythm. You then need to break that rhythm in order to hit a reload.

The five-second time limit for this drill is challenging, but reasonable. Just resist the temptation to slam a mag into the gun and then point your arms at the target and start whacking the trigger. Get a good sight picture. Pay attention to what you are doing. Make every shot count. Build good habits.

One thing that needs to be mentioned here as a bit of a reminder is that you should be preparing yourself for the possibility of trigger freeze when doing this sort of thing livefire. Pressing the trigger really hard during dryfire will help prepare you for the tension that builds during livefire.

One-Handed Shooting

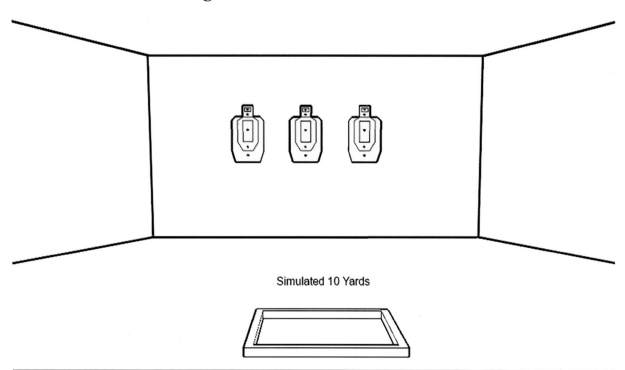

Simulated 10 Yards

Date:	Notes:

Procedure:

Start with your hands relaxed at sides or wrists above shoulders, facing downrange.

At the signal, draw and engage each target with two rounds either weak hand only or strong hand only.

I recommend that you alternate strong hand and weak hand every few repetitions.

Focus:

Develop the ability to shoot one-handed.

Goal:

Strong hand only, your par time is 2.2 seconds.

Weak hand only, your par time is 2.8 seconds.

Commentary:

Working on shooting with only one hand is something that can really give you a confidence boost when you see that challenge at an actual match.

One thing to pay attention to here is your grip pressure. People have a natural tendency to grip down even harder when shooting with only one hand. This does help with recoil control, but often people get in the habit of sympathetically tensing up their trigger finger along with the rest of their hand. Obviously, that is a very bad thing. Pay attention to moving your trigger finger independently of the rest of your hand and don't be shy about gripping down even harder when shooting with one hand. Dryfire is the perfect place to make this stuff subconscious.

If you are using a double-action pistol, you should also note that shooting with one hand makes that first shot even tougher. Take the time you need to press the trigger straight back. If you see the front sight wobble out of the notch during a double action press, then make some technique changes. I find it *feels* like it takes forever to press the trigger carefully enough, especially weak-handed, but that is only an issue of perception. If you are able to hit the goal times, you should be in good shape.

Plate Rack Drills

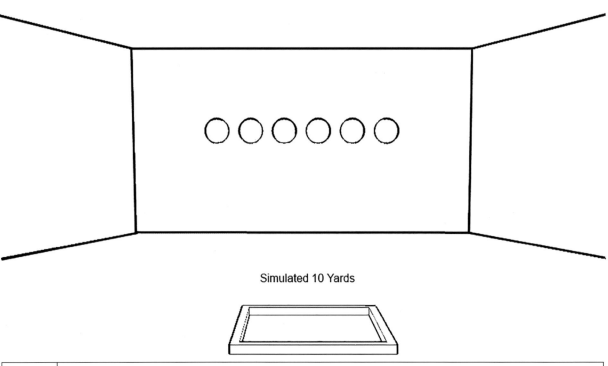

Simulated 10 Yards

Date:	Notes:

Setup Notes:

Bianchi plate racks are 8-inch plates spaced 20 inches apart, center to center. Set up your dry-fire rack to replicate those numbers.

Procedure:

Start with your hands relaxed at sides or wrists above shoulders, facing downrange. Engage each plate with one round.

Focus:

Become comfortable with shooting plate racks or similar scenarios.

Goal:

Freestyle, your par time is 2.3 seconds.

Strong hand only, your par time is 2.8 seconds.

Weak hand only, your par time is 3.5 seconds.

Commentary:

This drill requires that you construct a facsimile "plate rack." Essentially, you need to simulate eight inch plates at 10 yards.

I have included goal times for freestyle, strong hand only, and weak hand only. Obviously, I encourage you to try and hit each of those goal times.

Resist the temptation to "sweep" the plates. You may feel that the only way you can hit the plates in such a fast time is to keep the gun moving and keep pressing the trigger, but that is a habit that will be detrimental when you start shooting real bullets at the range. You should strive to see your sights pause on each plate as you engage them in turn. One alternate exercise you can try, if you are getting sucked in to "sweeping" the plates, is to remove all trigger presses from the equation and do the drill just getting a sight picture on each plate. Focus on a good sight picture in the center of each plate and then go to the next one. It should help with the "sweeping" problem.

Hitting the 2.3-second par time on this will require a bit of work and a bit of patience, but it is almost certainly doable. Work on breaking that first shot quickly. Work on hitting an aggressive pace across the plates. Work on being able to do it all consistently.

At the end of the day, it doesn't really matter that you be super quick on steel. What will make the difference is minimizing extra shots. Be mindful of this during your training. I like to build the habit of carefully calling every shot during my own practice, firing makeup shots as appropriate.

Distance Changeup

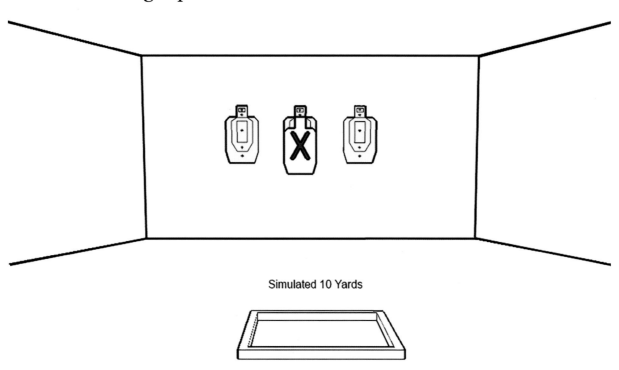

Simulated 10 Yards

Date:	Notes:

Procedure:

Start with your hands relaxed at sides or wrists above shoulders, facing downrange. Engage each target with two rounds.

Alternate your engagement order every few repetitions. Left to right, right to left, open targets, then the head box, and head box, then open targets are all options you should work with.

Focus:

Work on switching between different sight focal points.

Goal:

Your goal is a 2.3-second par time.

Commentary:

This drill absolutely relies on your own live-fire training. You need to know what your sights need to look like to hit the head shot. You need to know how carefully you must break the trigger. You also need to know what you can get away with on the open targets. Can you get "A" zone hits by shooting target focused? Do you just use your fiber dot? These are individual questions that you need to answer for yourself through experimentation on the range.

Once you have an idea of what you need to do, you can train yourself to do those things every single time in dryfire. You can develop the discipline to get a sharp front sight focus on the head box. For example, you can force yourself to push into the open targets using target focus.

The key to this drill is to develop the discipline you need to dial back and nail the tight shots every single time. You see that sort of challenge in matches frequently. You don't ever want to pick up a miss just because the target is a little bit tougher than the other targets on the stage.

Shooting While Moving

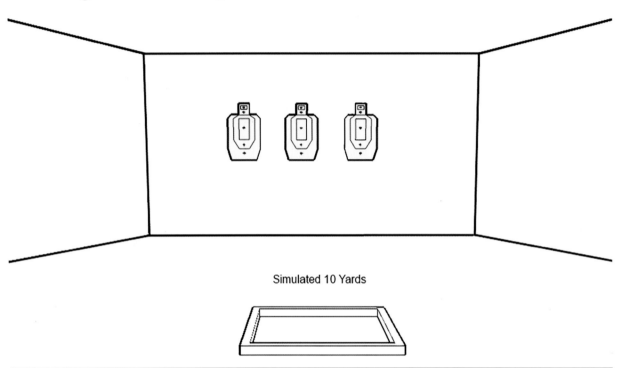

Simulated 10 Yards

Date:	Notes:

Procedure:

Start with your hands relaxed at sides or wrists above shoulders, facing squarely downrange. At the signal, engage each target with two rounds while you move in any desired direction. Alternate your direction of movement and starting hand position.

Focus:

Develop your ability to take shots while moving.

Goal:

Move three large steps and meet the 2.0-second par time while shooting the drill.

Commentary:

This drill is designed to help you improve your shooting while moving skills. These shots are easy enough that just about anyone ought to be able to make them while moving.

The first thing I need to point out is that the goal not only includes a time, but a distance. I don't really see the point of moving by taking small steps. When the situation calls for shooting while moving, I really like to make substantial movement. I don't want you to stop your movement during this drill if you happen to finish three steps before the conclusion of the par time. Instead, move right on through. The three steps are just a minimum of movement. Obviously, you may need to reconfigure your living space to make this work for you.

I also need to call your attention to the procedure for this drill. You may move in any desired direction. Please don't neglect training all the possibilities. Move forward, backward, left, right, and diagonally. You want to be prepared for any possibility.

The big caution here is that you need to be extremely careful with what you consider an appropriate sight picture. I like to see my sights appear rock solid as I move. As you learn to execute this skill, you are going to need to back it up with some live-fire to make sure what you are seeing in dryfire is actually appropriate. People have a tendency to let the sights bounce up and down as they move.

A good rule of thumb for taking targets while moving is to imagine that they are 50 percent further than their actual distance and get an appropriate sight picture for that. So, just pretend that these simulated 10-yard targets are actually set at 15 yards.

Shooting While Moving Hard

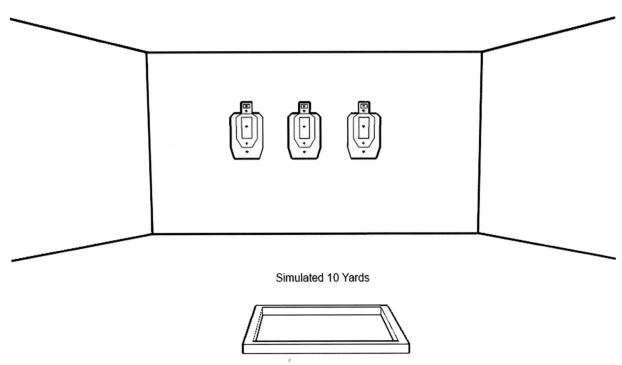

Simulated 10 Yards

Date:	Notes:

Procedure:

Start with your hands relaxed at sides or wrists above shoulders, facing squarely downrange. At the signal, engage the head box of each target with two rounds while you move in any desired direction. Alternate your direction of movement and starting hand position. You may substitute a partial target in the place of using the head box. The head box is used for convenience.

Focus:

Develop your ability to take difficult/risky shots while moving.

Goal:

Move three large steps and meet the 3.5-second par time while shooting the drill.

Commentary:

This drill is essentially the same idea as the prior shooting while moving drill, but it is done using much more challenging targets.

The important point here is that this drill is designed to really challenge you. Keep in mind that these targets are difficult enough that it may not make sense to shoot them while moving in an actual match situation, but for the purposes of practice it does make sense to push yourself to the absolute limit.

Pay close attention to your sight picture for each shot and try to see where your sights are at all times. If you see your sights dip into the no-shoot target, you can even fire an extra shot on the shoot target to make it up.

Of course, you should feel free to modify this drill. Use no-shoots, hard cover, different targets, and any other element you feel adds to the challenge or makes things more interesting.

Quick Step

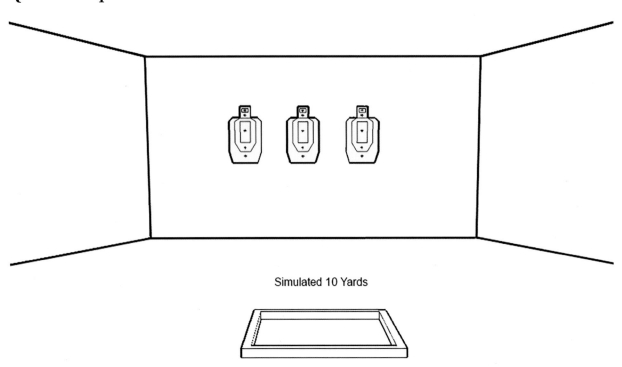

Simulated 10 Yards

Date:	Notes:

Setup Notes:

This drill requires a one-yard square shooting box.

Procedure:

Start facing downrange, standing *outside* of the box with one of your feet touching the box. Start with your hands relaxed at sides or wrists above shoulders. At the signal, engage each target with two rounds. After firing your sixth round, move directly *across* the box. Once you have crossed the box you engage one target with an additional two rounds. This may be any target you desire.

You are not allowed to actually be in the box while firing any rounds.

For clarity, if you don't quite understand what I mean by "crossing" the box, you are to go from standing outside one part of the box to standing outside the box on the opposite side.

You may reverse the engagement order. Instead of firing six rounds, then moving, then firing two rounds, you may fire two rounds, then move, then fire six rounds.

Focus:
Work on making quick little movements.

Goal:
Your goal is a 3.5-second par time.

Commentary:
This drill is designed to develop your ability to make a short movement in an explosive, but controlled fashion. You see this sometimes in matches and the dynamics are a bit different than scenarios where you have more space to run.

As you work through this drill, you should play around with gun positioning during the movement. You don't want to drop down too much because you are going to need to get right back up on target less than a second after you get moving. You also don't want to stay fully extended because the gun bounces around uncontrollably if you move aggressively. Some experimentation on your part is absolutely key.

I encourage you to work this drill in every possible movement direction, including diagonally. You want to be comfortable moving any direction that may be required of you. I want to point out that you are going to be just a hair slower moving backward and that shouldn't concern you much. It is normal to not be able to move backward as fast as you can move other directions. Just be aware that I did not set the par time for backward movement, so if you can't quite hit it, you shouldn't worry.

If you wish, you can work a reload into the drill as you move. Again, I didn't set the par time for this, so you may well end up being a hair slower if you work in a reload.

Part 6

SCENARIOS

This section contains instructions for setting up training scenarios. These scenarios by nature are not things that will be pegged with a specific par time. I will leave it up to you to set par times and work to reduce them if you wish. These scenarios include things like position entry and exit, dealing with ports, working around barricades, and seated starts. Think about it like this: essentially every single shooting skill you are likely to find at a match is contained in this section. All you do is recreate these challenges to the best of your ability in your dryfire space and work through them, building technique and comfort as you do it.

It is important to point out how important it is for you to be able to improvise as you recreate these scenarios. Walls inside your house can become vision barriers; you can construct barricades; you could even put down some sort of marker on the ground to indicate a shooting position. Creativity is really important when you are looking to train for scenarios that will take place on an outdoor range, but you are only using a limited indoor space. Most people simply don't have a big area in which to dryfire practice.

Since you will be improvising these exercises to work in your own training space, I can't give you specific time goals. Instead of that, I will provide technical pointers. You should pay careful attention to these items as you work through these scenarios in order to train to the greatest effect. Over time, you should be building familiarity and comfort with various shooting challenges. When you go to a match it shouldn't be the only time you reload from a table or get into the prone position. These scenarios can help prepare you for actual competition and as such you shouldn't neglect them.

I encourage you to become at least familiar with all these scenarios. You don't need to practice every scenario, every day. That isn't possible. However, you should rotate through these scenarios in turn, so that you work on everything at least a little bit every month. I would focus more on the normal movement and transition scenarios and do the more obscure things, like prone shooting and picking magazines up off a table, on a more occasional basis.

One very important note as far as setup of these scenarios is concerned: Do not try to replicate the diagram. What you should be doing is replicating the *challenge*. If the drill calls for two shooting positions, then you can construct them as you wish. Move left to right, right to left, front to back, etc. Change the distance of the movements involved. You need to train yourself for everything, so please don't neglect doing that. You are free to work in a requirement to reload on the movement drills here, even if the drill doesn't call for it. The variations are endless, so make sure you try to bring endless variation to your training.

Position Entry

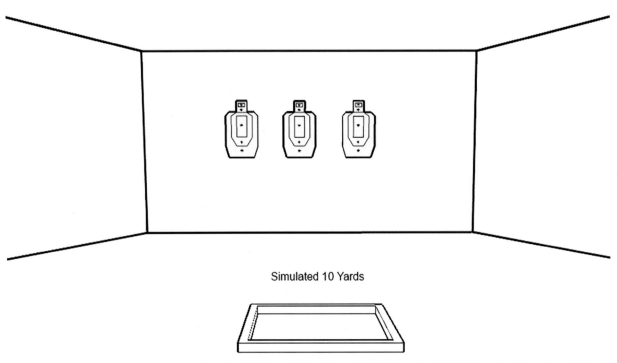

Simulated 10 Yards

Date:	Notes:

Procedure:

Start in the position with a single target. Draw and engage that target, then move to the next position. Engage all targets from that position. Set a par time and work to reduce it.

Focus:

Work on getting into position with the gun ready to fire.

Goal:

Your goal is to set up into the second position with the gun up and ready to fire. You should be stopped and stable, ready to shoot, immediately upon entering the second position. Minimize extraneous movements, like standing up taller or shuffling your feet.

Commentary:

The point of this drill is to get used to the sensation of having your gun up and ready to shoot when you come into a position.

Many shooters put their gun up in front of their face and then feel they have accomplished the task. I don't think this is the right way to do it. The idea is to not only have your gun up, but to be *ready*. The best way I know to be ready is to be aiming down the sights at the first target you plan to shoot. Keep fighting to stabilize your sight picture. When the sights are stable enough, you should start firing.

If you feel a specific technique is best in terms of how to set your feet and what foot to use to enter the shooting area first or anything along those lines, be aware that dryfire practice is the best place to learn that skill and make it subconscious. Once you have it down at home, take it to the range and see how you stack up.

After every repetition, I find it helpful to check my stance. This means when you finish a rep you should stop moving and consciously look down at your feet and check your muscle tension. You want a nice wide and stable stance. You want a 50/50 weight distribution so you aren't leaned up to one side. The thinking here is that when you stop in your shooting position, you should be ready to move to the next one. Long courses at matches will have many positions, not just two. Your training should reflect that reality.

You should vary this scenario by changing up the target difficulty. I suggest beginning your training on more difficult targets. Partial targets, or the like, require that you get completely stopped and stable in order to get an acceptable sight picture on them. This will make it difficult for you to have sloppy technique with good results. As you grow in skill, you will likely want to learn to shoot targets earlier and earlier as you come into position. This means you may be engaging targets before you even get stopped.

Position Exit

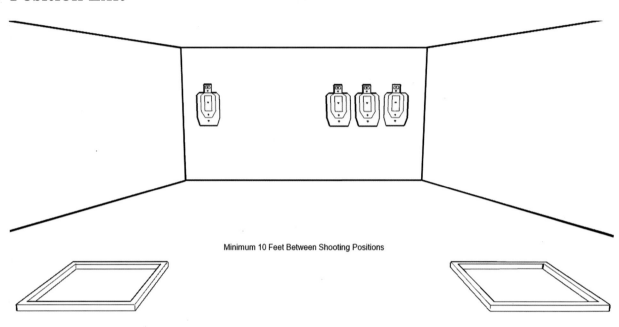

Minimum 10 Feet Between Shooting Positions

Date:	Notes:

Procedure:

Start in the position with multiple targets. Draw and engage those targets, then explosively move to the next position. Get the gun up and ready to go and engage the target in that position. Set a par time and work to reduce it.

Focus:

Work on aggressively and explosively getting out of position.

Goal:

Push yourself out of position, using all the muscles you can in both legs. Get yourself up to your top possible movement speed.

Commentary:

On this drill, you are working on getting out of position explosively. I like to strive for a feeling of pushing with both my feet to get out of position. I want to use all the muscles at my disposal to exit that initial shooting position.

I think you should begin your training on relatively tough targets. These should help force you to stay completely stopped and stable in position until the precise moment it is time to leave. At the instant you call that last shot, you put everything you have into moving out of position.

As you develop your skills, you can make the targets easier and easier. On closer-range targets, it is sometimes appropriate to "cheat" a little bit and start leaning out of position as you fire the last couple shots. Of course, this is something that requires practice to pull off consistently and dryfire affords you the opportunity to do that. I like to do this "lean" technique without picking up my feet. As soon as a foot comes off the ground, it disrupts your balance, and you can't then use that foot to push yourself to the next position.

The most common mistake to watch out for here is the tendency to leave your shooting position early. This happens normally when you start to push down on the par time. Just be aware that you are to shoot, and *then* move. You do each thing as fast as you can do it and don't try to do them at the same time. It is only later on in your training that you start "cheating" with the lean out of position technique, or some similar strategy.

Port

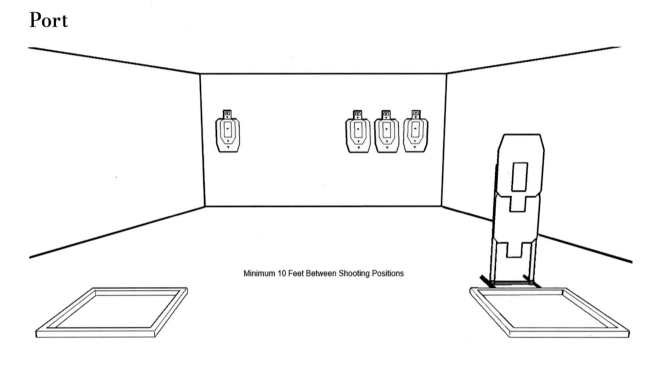

Minimum 10 Feet Between Shooting Positions

Date:	Notes:

Setup Notes:

This drill requires you to construct a shooting port. You are free to construct it out of anything you want. I personally prefer to use a couple full-size targets and a full-size target stand. I just cut the "A" zone from a target and use the hole as my shooting port.

The port for this drill should be constructed at a height you find comfortable to shoot from. You shouldn't need to crouch down to shoot through the port.

Procedure:

Start in the position with a single target. Engage that target and then move to the port. Engage all required targets through the port. This drill should also be done with the positions in reverse order. Set a par time and work to reduce it.

Focus:

Learn to get set up to shoot through a port. Learn also to exit the port.

Goal:

Set up in the port wide and stable to efficiently engage the targets. Learn also to aggressively exit the port. Set a par time and work to reduce it.

Commentary:

This drill is designed to help you get comfortable setting up in ports. Ports are an interesting challenge because you will need to have the gun up and in position before you can actually see the target. You need to get comfortable with aiming through vision barriers. Don't wait until you can engage a target to start aiming at it; you are wasting time doing that. Start aiming before you can engage it, so as soon as the target becomes available, you are ready to whack it.

Normal principals like getting stopped and stable apply here. The port shouldn't make much difference in that respect. What will make a difference is that you set up so you can engage all the targets through the port without moving your feet, if that is at all possible given the scenario that you build. You don't want unnecessary foot shuffling as you try to shoot through the port. It will disrupt and destabilize your sight picture.

Make sure that you work this drill backward as well. Start in the port and then practice getting out of it. Be sure to work on both easy targets that you can shoot as you move and tough targets that require you be stopped and stabilized.

Low Port

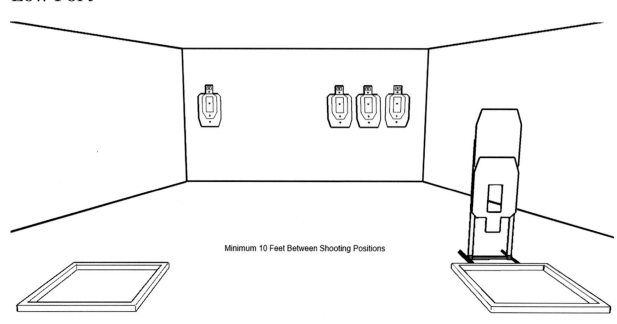

Minimum 10 Feet Between Shooting Positions

Date:	Notes:

Setup Notes:

This drill requires you to construct a shooting port. You are free to construct it out of anything you want. I personally prefer to use a couple full-size targets and a full-size target stand. I just cut the "A" zone from a target and use the hole as my shooting port.

The port for this drill should be constructed at a height that presents a reasonable challenge for you. The port needs to be low down enough that you need to get into a very low squat or drop to a knee. The port shouldn't be so low that you are tempted to go prone.

Procedure:

Start in the position with a single target. Engage that target and then move to the port. Engage all required targets through the port. This drill should also be done with the positions in reverse order. Set a par time and work to reduce it.

Focus:

Learn to get set up to shoot through a low port. Learn also to exit the low port.

Goal:

Set up in the port low and stable to efficiently engage the targets. Learn also to aggressively exit the port. Set a par time and work to reduce it.

Commentary:

This is a good drill to save for toward the end of a practice session. If you are doing it right, it is going to take a lot out of your legs. For that reason, this is a good one to end on for the day.

One thing I want you to experiment with is getting down to one knee, versus getting down to a squat. If you are using a par time, you will probably see there is not much of a difference in the time it takes to get down to one positions, versus the other. Of course, getting out of that position will be a different story.

Another thing you should play around with is the gun position as you get down low. If the gun is fully extended, you may find that it bounces around as you get low, especially if you go down to a knee as opposed to a squat. This is a phenomenon you should learn to manage in dryfire, so when you get on the range for real, you can just worry about the noisy part.

Barricade

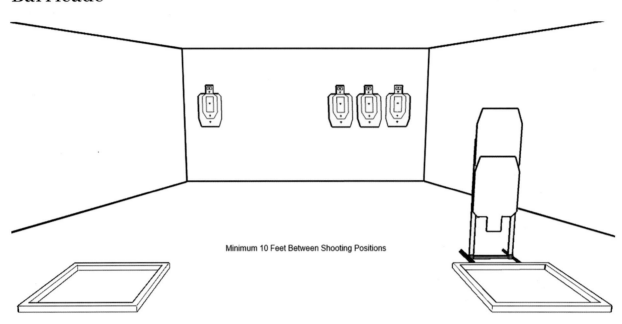

Minimum 10 Feet Between Shooting Positions

Date:	Notes:

Setup Notes:

This drill requires you to construct a shooting barricade. You are free to construct it out of anything you want. I personally prefer to use a couple full-size targets and a full-size target stand.

You should construct a box connected to the barricade in order to force yourself to actually stand behind the barricade and shoot around it.

Procedure:

Start in the position with a single target. Engage that target and then move to the barricade. Engage all required targets from around the barricade. This drill should also be done with the positions in reverse order. Set a par time and work to reduce it.

Focus:

Learn to quickly get set up to shoot around a barricade. Learn also to exit the barricade position.

Goal:

Set up around the barricade wide and stable to efficiently engage the targets. Learn also to aggressively exit the barricade position. Set a par time and work to reduce it.

Commentary:

First, I want to point out that all of the concerns with the par time that I presented in the previous "Port Entry" drill absolutely apply to this one. You need to have the gun up early and be able to aim right through vision barriers at the targets.

This drill is designed to help you learn to get set up to shoot around barricades. Usually, I don't really worry too much about my specific foot positioning, but when you start working with a really constricted shooting area behind a barricade, things can get tricky. You need to have some sort of a plan for how you are going to get your feet into the correct position. If you have any questions about how you need to do this, I suggest you work backward. Just stand in your shooting area and lean around your barricade in very comfortable fashion. As soon as you have figured out how you want your feet and body to end up, you should have an easier time working out how to end up that way.

Prone

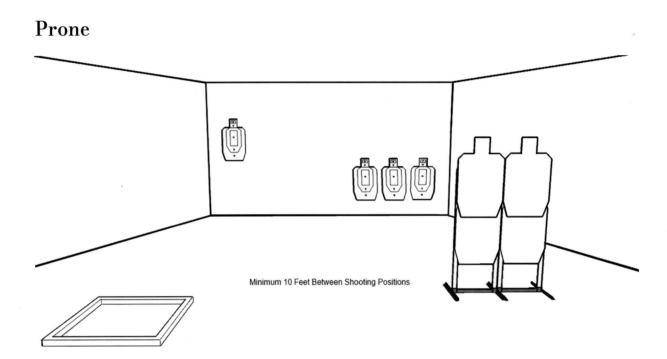

Minimum 10 Feet Between Shooting Positions

Date:	Notes:

Setup Notes:

Make a note of the wall section in the drill diagram. You can construct a similar wall section and force yourself to shoot under it if you want the same visual effect that you will likely see at a match. It may be more work than it is worth, so feel free to work on prone shooting without the wall section.

You may also want to make a note that the targets are placed lower on the wall for prone shooting practice. Because of the way ranges are constructed, you will infrequently need to do prone shooting at an upward angle. Most ranges don't have berms high enough to allow extreme upward angles. Just be aware of this fact and construct your at home training to be something plausible for a match situation.

Procedure:

Start in the position with a single target. Engage that target and then move to the prone position. Then engage all required targets while prone. This drill should also be done with the positions in reverse order. When you start at the position that requires prone shooting, start standing, go prone after you draw, then move to the other position. Set a par time and work to reduce it.

Focus:

Learn to quickly get set up to shoot from the prone position. Learn also to exit the prone position.

Goal:

Set up in the prone position efficiently. Learn also to aggressively exit the prone position. Set a par time and work to reduce it.

Commentary:

Prone shooting is a bit of an uncommon challenge to see in matches these days, but it is still something you may occasionally see. The idea behind this drill is to take the time to figure out how to go prone.

You have a few technical options here. Some shooters are able to virtually throw themselves onto the ground and get to shooting. Other shooters put a hand on the ground, then lower themselves down. Obviously, the better shape you are in, the more of an advantage you are going to have when it comes to getting down prone.

The other thing to pay attention to is being able to transition between the targets. Depending on how you set things up, it may be difficult for you to go from one target to the other. This is a common challenge with prone shooting and it is something you need to be prepared for. You may well have to reposition your whole body just to transition! Be ready for that stuff.

Finally, you need to train this scenario in reverse order. It can happen in a match that you are required to get up from the prone position, and you need to be ready for that. I recommend getting your non-firing hand on the ground and using it to aggressively push yourself up and out of that position.

Up and Down Transitions

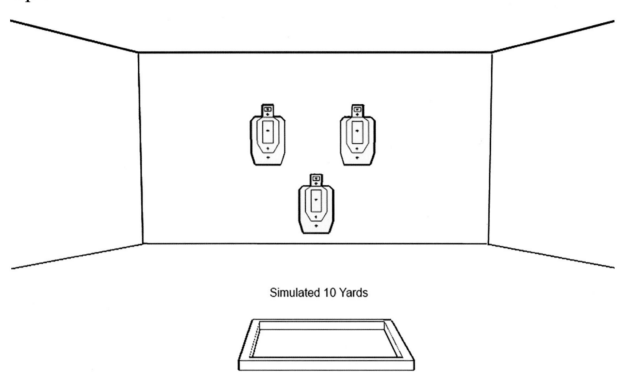

Simulated 10 Yards

Date:	Notes:

Setup Notes:

Depending on the scale of targets you are using, you may need to adjust the height of the targets on the wall. With small-scale targets, you will be standing so close to the wall that you may not want to have the low target near the floor. If you are using larger scale, you may need to have the bottom of the target touching the floor in order to create the proper effect for the drill. Do some experimentation to figure it out.

Procedure:

Engage each target with two rounds. Alternate which target you engage first. Set a par time and work to reduce it.

Focus:

Develop strong up and down transitions.

Goal:

Your goal is to be able to engage the targets in any order and have nice "clean" gun movement from one to the other. Be wary of pushing the gun around too hard.

Commentary:

Transitioning the gun up and down is a common challenge and it is one you want to prepare for.

I think the biggest challenge with transitions like this is that your arms can actually be in the way of your vision of the low target. This doesn't necessarily screw things up; it can just be a little bit disconcerting.

For this reason, the procedure of this drill requires you to alternate which target you engage first. Make sure you try every possible combination of target engagement order, including going low target first. I think many shooters will probably find that they prefer going low target first because it will avoid that uncomfortable transition down to the low target.

Obviously, in a match scenario you will not always get to start on the low targets. There may be some other factors causing you to pick a different order. For that reason, you need to be comfortable with every possibility.

90-Degree Transitions

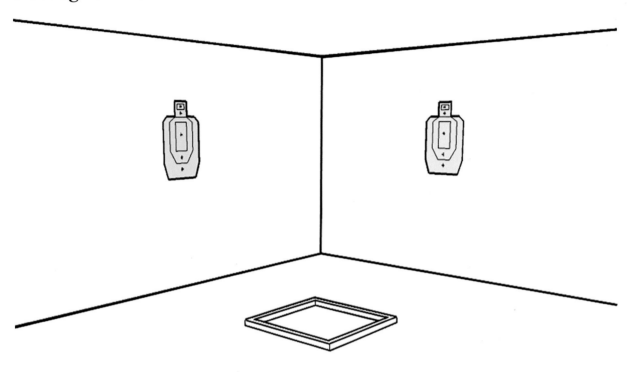

Date:	Notes:

Setup Notes:

Due to this drill using the corner of a room to simulate transition angles, it is difficult to actually specify distances for the targets. Set this up so you get the full 90 degrees of swing between targets.

Procedure:

Start with your hands relaxed at sides, facing directly downrange. Engage each target with two rounds. Alternate which target you engage first. Set a par time and work to reduce it.

Focus:

Work on wide transitions.

Goal:

You want "clean" transitions between each target.

Commentary:

Wide transitions are a fact of life in USPSA competition. This drill is the easiest variation of wide transitions that you will find in this book. The targets are relatively easy; you shouldn't have a hard time really powering the gun between the targets.

On this drill, you may feel a sensation of having the transition come from your legs. I think that is a good thing and it may help you be a bit faster from target to target. The reality of the way stages are actually set up means you will not often feel that sensation in an actual match. That having been said, I think you should get a feel for getting your feet set in position and using your legs to transition.

As always, with these high-speed transition drills, you need to be exceedingly careful to make sure you aren't pulling the gun off target early or getting on the trigger too soon as you transition over to the next target. Doing a little bit of livefire training on drills like this will help confirm you have done your dryfire correctly.

180-Degree Transitions

Date:	Notes:

Setup Notes:

Due to this drill using the corners of a room to simulate transition angles, it is difficult to actually specify distances for the targets. Set the targets so you have a 180-degree transition between them.

Procedure:

Start with your hands relaxed at sides, facing directly downrange. Engage each target with two rounds. Alternate which target you engage first. Sct a par time and work to reduce it.

Focus:

Work on extremely wide transitions.

Goal:

You want "clean" transitions between each target.

Commentary:

Obviously, due to USPSA safety rules, you shouldn't ever see a truly 180-degree transition. It would be right up against the limit of what the rules would allow, and would almost certainly result in some match disqualifications. That having been said, you will probably encounter very wide transitions on a regular basis.

The start position stipulates that you must start facing directly downrange. Please don't cheat on this. You are required to start basically favoring neither target. As you can imagine, there is a bit of footwork that will likely be required in order for you to expeditiously engage each target. You could try to engage the targets without moving your feet. You could also square up to each target as you engage it in turn. Your preference will depend on how you are built physically. Experiment with the footwork and figure out something that works.

In terms of transition technique, I strongly recommend that you pull the gun in close to your body when you transition to the second target. Of course, this book isn't about shooting technique, but pulling the gun in close on wide transitions is critical to your success on this drill, so I can't neglect to mention it.

Finally, there is the issue of the draw. You may find it quite uncomfortable to draw on this drill, especially when you need to draw across your body to engage the target to your left (for a right-handed shooter). Drawing at strange angles like this is a bit disconcerting, but you need to be prepared for it. Drive the gun on target as aggressively as you can, pay attention to safety rules and avoid sweeping yourself, and hit that goal time as consistently as you can.

Gun Pickup

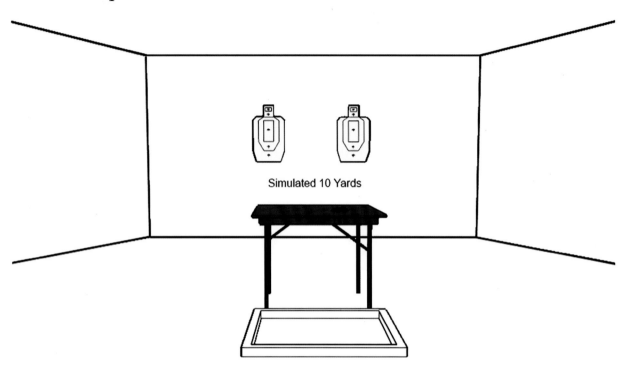

Simulated 10 Yards

Date:	Notes:

Setup Notes:

This drill requires a table to set your gun on. A folding card table works well if you have access to one.

Procedure:

Start standing uprange of the table. At the signal, pick up your pistol and engage each target with two rounds. Set a par time and work to reduce it.

Focus:

Become proficient picking your gun up from a table and then engaging targets.

Goal:

Your goal is a perfect grip as you bring the gun up.

Commentary:

This drill is good practice for the scenarios where you need to pick your gun up and then engage targets immediately. You encounter this sort of thing in matches occasionally, and it never hurts to practice it. As you might expect, the most important element to pay attention to is your grip consistency. You need to build up a solid grip, but do so quickly.

One thing you can mess around with is the surface of the table. You could use a wood table and then put a tablecloth on it after a few repetitions. You may notice some differences when you work off of a cloth. If you have a scrap of carpet available, that may be worth trying as well. You may find it makes it more difficult to effectively grip your gun if you have carpet in the way.

Get your grip on the gun, get on target, and get your hits.

Ammo Pickup

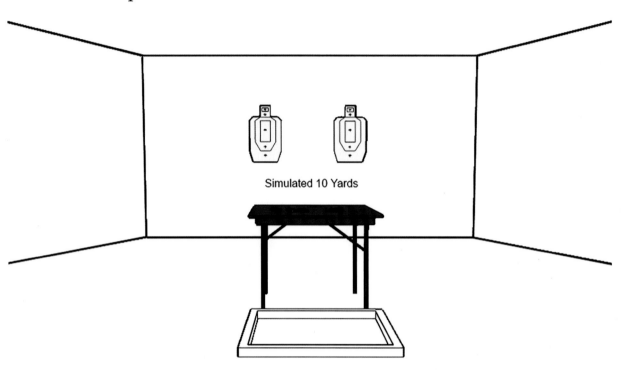

Simulated 10 Yards

Date:	Notes:

Setup Notes:

This drill requires a table to set your gun and magazines on. A folding card table works well if you have access to one.

Procedure:

Start anywhere you like. Your gun and magazines should be set on the table. Make sure you have your muzzle pointed downrange. Your gun must be *unloaded*.

Drill One:

At the signal, load your gun and engage each target with two rounds. Set a par time and work to reduce it.

Drill Two:

At the signal, load your gun and engage each target with two rounds. You must also pick up two additional magazines and retain them on your body. You may perform these things in any order, but at the stop beep you must have accomplished all of the required actions. Set a par time and work to reduce it.

Focus:

Work at picking up ammunition off a table.

Goal:

Be comfortable and consistent when it comes to handling your gun and ammunition from a table.

Commentary:

It is not at all an uncommon situation that you will be required to start with your gun unloaded and the ammunition placed on a table or a barrel. This drill should prepare you for that scenario.

The first drill is to simply load the gun and engage the targets. I recommend you pay attention to how you set the gun on the table in the first place. Pay attention to how you place the magazines. You need to be able to grab them properly. You should also consider how high to bring the gun up before you attempt to load it. Loading down at crotch level can be difficult. These are all ideas to consider as you work through the drill.

Drill Two has the same requirement to load the gun and engage targets, but it adds in the stipulation that you stow two magazines away. This sort of thing does happen occasionally at matches and you need to be ready for it, especially if you shoot a low-capacity division where you may need to retain four or five magazines to finish a big stage.

Remember that it doesn't matter what order you do things in. You can load and shoot, then stuff magazines or you can do the opposite. You can even do half of one thing, then the other thing, then back to the first thing. It doesn't matter. Just get everything done within the goal time. I think you will learn quite a bit during this type of practice, so you will not have to worry about these elements when you see them at a match. You will have figured out the most efficient way for you to do things.

Finally, you can make these drills harder by setting your gun and mags on the table in undesirable spots. Some matches make you put the magazines all in one corner of the table, or some other stipulation, and it can be pretty annoying. Make sure you try that sort of thing during your own training.

Seated Start

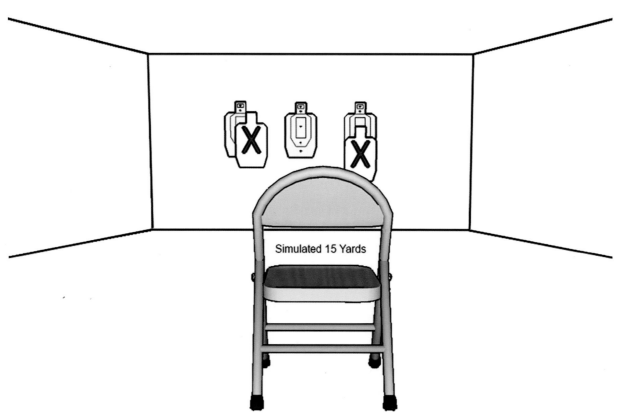

Simulated 15 Yards

Date:	Notes:

Setup Notes:

This drill requires a chair. A folding chair is a prop that you can expect to see in matches, so that is probably the best choice. If that isn't available, just make sure you have a chair that doesn't have excessive cushioning that will prevent you from standing up.

Procedure:

Start seated, with your butt completely on the chair and your hands on your knees. At the signal, draw and engage each target with two rounds. Set a par time and work to reduce it.

Focus:

Learn to draw your pistol and stand up efficiently.

Goal:

Your goal is to stand up quickly and get a clean grip on your pistol.

Commentary:

A common start position at USPSA matches is the seated start. There isn't any real trick to this, it is just something you need to get used to. I think it is almost always desirable to stand up as you draw in a USPSA setting, so the rest of my comments will address that contingency.

The toughest thing to do correctly is to nail your draw. As soon as you start standing up it will start moving your holster. That can be a challenging thing to get used to. The easiest way to handle it is to stay seated until you get your strong hand on the gun. If you choose to start standing right away and not wait to get on the gun, you will likely get a faster first shot, but it will be tough to nail your grip.

Notice that the target scenario for this drill includes two challenging partial targets and one open target. This is intentional. You may well find that it is easier for you to engage the open target first because you will not need to be as stable in order to fire good shots on it. You could take a partial target first, but you may find that you need to fight to stabilize your sight picture on it a bit more than the open target.

There are a couple of safety issues I should call your attention to.

First, be extra careful of your muzzle direction as you draw. USPSA rules currently allow you to sweep your leg as you draw, but I think it is fair to say that it is not a "best practice" sort of thing. If you have a problem with sweeping your legs when you draw your pistol, then take advantage of your dryfire training to build different habits.

The other issue is the possibility of getting the gear on the back of your belt caught in the chair. There are several YouTube videos floating around where a USPSA competitor shoots a stage with a folding chair caught on his belt. Obviously, that is the kind of thing that can cause you to fall over or possibly rip your belt off putting your gear on the ground. You don't want to be the next YouTube superstar, so start paying attention to this stuff in dryfire. You should prepare yourself for the possibility that you will be required to start with your back against the back of a folding chair. Usually, I just make sure not to have a magazine in any of my rear pouches in order to minimize the possibility of getting snagged. The stage may require enough shots that you don't have the option to run light on ammo. Having your back against the back of a folding chair with a full belt is basically a worst-case scenario. Make sure you can get through that without getting caught on the chair! Take a bit of extra time if you need to.

Prop Manipulation

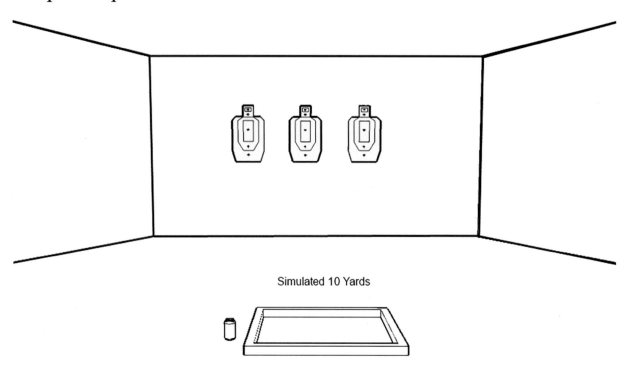

Simulated 10 Yards

Date:	Notes:

Setup Notes:

This drill requires a prop for you to mess around with. I prefer to use an empty soda can. You are welcome to use anything you like.

The shooting area can be whatever size you like, but it will be important for you to mark off the edges of the shooting area.

Procedure:

Start with your hands relaxed at sides, standing in the box, facing downrange. Have your soda can (or whatever) placed outside the box on the left. Engage each target with two rounds, then reload, then move the can from the left to the right. After the can is placed outside the shooting area on the right side, engage each target with an additional two rounds.

You can vary this drill by moving the can from front to back, right to left, and back to front.

Set a par time and work to reduce it.

Focus:

Work on dealing with props during shooting a stage.

Goal:

Your goal is to smoothly, efficiently, and consistently deal with the prop.

Commentary:

This drill may strike some as a little bit silly. I understand that soda cans are not a terribly common prop in USPSA competition. The can is just a stand in. It represents a lever, a rope, an ammo can, or anything else that a match director could potentially make you mess around with at some point during a stage.

The whole idea is that you are shooting, then you mess around with the prop as quickly and efficiently as you can, then you get back to the shooting. Your key to all of this is doing a little bit of mental rehearsal before you execute the drill. You want the prop manipulation part of the drill to be just as smooth as a reload or a draw. It should appear to a casual observer just like business as usual.

You will note that there isn't a goal time for this drill. Due to the different variations, there are for this drill, I think it would be counterproductive to have you pushing a goal time. Instead, make sure that you feel smooth and controlled during the drill. Make sure that messing around with the soda can doesn't force any mistakes. Once you are able to consistently execute like that, you should be able to move on to the next thing.

Part 7
ASSORTED EXERCISES

"Assorted Exercises" are drills that don't cleanly fit into any other section. These have different requirements and focal points when compared to the other more traditional stuff. Pay very careful attention to the setup notes and procedure for these because they really do their own thing.

To be honest, the point of most of these drills is to add a bit of variety and fun to your dryfire training. For example, having a drill where you simply run back and forth changing magazines is a good way to test yourself to make sure your training is OK, and it can be a fun way to blow off steam toward the end of a dryfire session.

If your dryfire is in a rut and you are looking for something a little bit different to mess around with, then these drills will probably do the trick just fine.

Widening Transitions

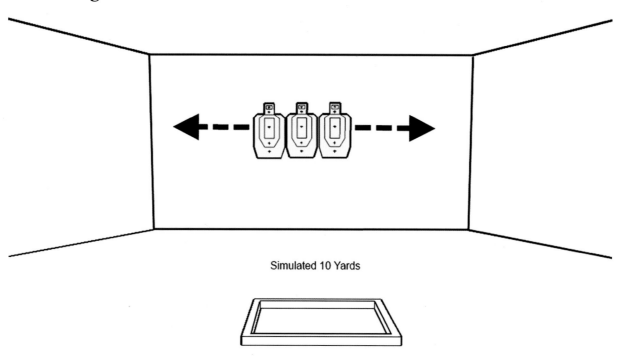

Simulated 10 Yards

Date:	Notes:

Procedure:

Set the targets so they have no space between them. They should be touching, edge to edge. Establish a par time for engaging each target with two rounds. Every few repetitions you should widen the target spacing out slightly without adjusting the par time. Continue on in this fashion until you are unable to meet the par time.

Focus:

Speed up transition times and learn to spot transition errors.

Goal:

Get the targets as far apart as possible while still meeting the par time. Observe the point where you are unable to complete the drill in the par time and work to correct it. You should have a good grasp of your errors.

Special Instructions:

This drill has the unusual stipulation of requiring you to move the targets as you progress through the drill. You initially start with the targets touching each other. You then start widening out the transitions by moving the outside two targets further away from the center target, thus increasing the transition distance. The diagram should show you how you move the targets. You start with the three targets touching. As you progress, you move the outside targets further away from the center target as the diagram shows.

A possible variation is to move the center target down lower and lower as you progress, forcing you to have a down and then up transition.

Commentary:

In case it isn't perfectly clear what the procedure for this drill is, let me clarify. You start with the three targets touching each other. You then set your par time to shoot those targets in that position. Without adjusting the par time, you start moving the targets further apart (widening the transition). You keep widening the targets in this fashion, every few repetitions of the drill, until you hit your limit.

This drill is designed as a skill builder for those that are already fairly proficient at moving from target to target, but are looking for a bit more speed. Like any transition drill, make sure you aren't pulling off target too soon or getting on the trigger before you get on the next target. This drill can be dangerous for newer shooters because, by definition, you are going to be pushed to the breaking point. You need to have the self-awareness to realize that you have hit that breaking point and stop yourself from building bad habits.

Skip Rope

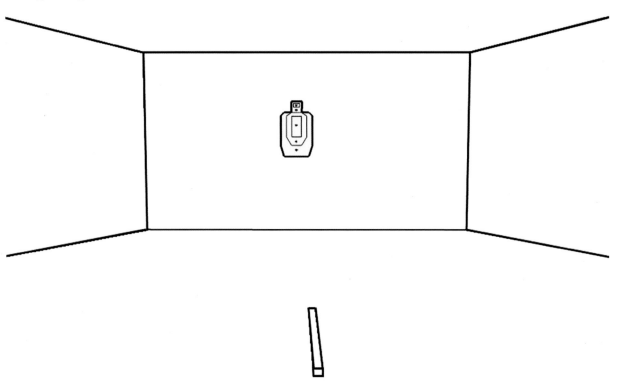

Date:	Notes:

Procedure:

Lay down a marking on the floor that is perpendicular to the backstop/target. I prefer to use a piece of rope or target stick, but feel free to use anything you have available. Start standing completely on one side or the other of that marking. At the start signal, draw and get a sight picture on the target. After you have that sight picture, push yourself completely to the opposite side of your line. After you have both feet on the floor on the opposite side of the line, get a sight picture on the target again. Then repeat this process, moving back to the opposite side of the line and getting a sight picture. Make four movements like this as quickly as you can. This is a total of five sight pictures (including the draw). Set a par time and work to reduce it.

Focus:

Work on being able to make quick movements and maintain stability.

Goal:

Gain the ability to aggressively push from one position to another and maintain stability. The ideal situation is that you are able to push with both feet as hard as you can and move across your marking on the floor. While you are doing that, you are able to maintain a workable sight picture on the target. A reasonable par time is 4.0 seconds.

Commentary:

Just to make sure there is clarity here, all you are really doing is getting a sight picture on the target then pushing across the line and getting another sight picture. You repeat this process for four movements back and forth across that line.

As far as technical focus, you need to hold the gun up high and be ready to get a clean sight picture on the target. Dropping the gun down will cost you time as you need to bring it back up. I have experimented quite a lot and if the gun substantially lowers it definitely hurts my time on this drill.

Another thing to pay attention to here is keeping a wide stance as much as you can. It is hard to stop yourself from getting crowded up on the marker on the ground. By this I mean you need to move far across the line to give yourself room to set up in to a proper stance. That can be very tough to do, but make that effort.

Finally, don't "cheat" the drill. You need to push all the way across the line, get a good sight picture, and get both feet planted for a rep to "count." If you cut corners on that you are ultimately damaging your own training. Please don't do that!

Skip Rope Reloads

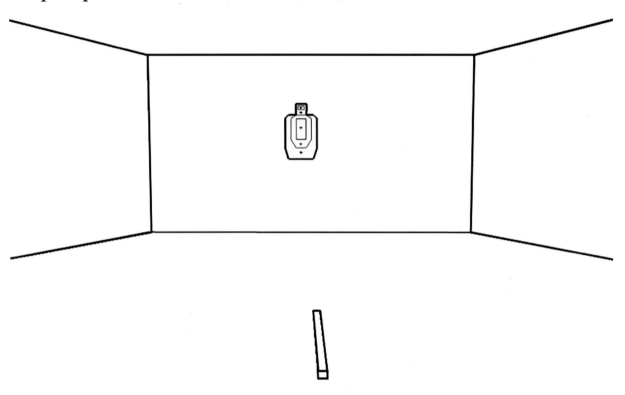

Date:	Notes:

Procedure:

Lay down a marking on the floor that is perpendicular to the backstop/target. I prefer to use a piece of rope or target stick, but feel free to use anything you have available. Start standing completely on one side or the other of that marking. At the start signal, draw and get a sight picture on the target. After you have that sight picture, push yourself completely to the opposite side of your line and reload. You will move back and forth like this, reloading each time. Make four movements, with reloads, like this as quickly as you can. This is a total of five sight pictures (including the draw). Set a par time and work to reduce it.

Focus:

Work on being able to make quick movements and get the gun reloaded in a small space.

Goal:

Gain the ability to aggressively push from one position to another. Learn to balance movement aggression with your ability to get the gun reloaded. The more aggressive the movement, the harder it is to reload quickly. Goal par time is 6.0 seconds.

Commentary:

This drill is obviously the same as the preceding "Skip Rope," except you are adding a reload in on every movement.

This is a common scenario for low-capacity divisions. It is frequently the case that you will need to reload, but essentially only have one or two steps between firing positions. This drill does a good job of replicating the challenge.

The main issue here is to perhaps move a bit less aggressively and get that reload done. Make sure you direct your attention to the gun as you are getting the reload done. This means you need to shift your attention from the target, down to the gun, and then back up again.

Personally, I really work to be patient during this drill. It will feel like it takes an eternity to get the reload done, and with a target right in your face, you will likely be tempted to rush to get back on target and start scoring some points. The reload may feel slow, but it probably won't be if your technique is good. Just make sure you have nice clean execution and get back on target as soon as the magazine is in the gun.

Running Reloads

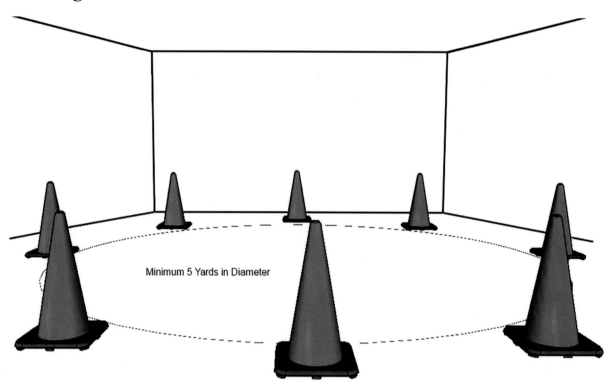

Minimum 5 Yards in Diameter

Date:	Notes:

Procedure:

Set up a circular pattern of markers on the ground. Run around the circle at top speed while executing a reload every 2 or 3 seconds. Go through all the magazines on your belt.

Focus:

Get comfortable with running top speed and executing reloads while you do it.

Goal:

Gain the ability to run flat out and execute clean reloads.

Commentary:

In normal situations, you are static while you shoot, and then can find your next magazine while you are moving out of position before you get a lot of speed built up. However, in some scenarios you are going to get a good bit of momentum built up as you move through a stage and will need to execute a reload during that time. This can happen on stages with lots of movement and very close-range targets. This drill will help you get comfortable executing a reload fully on the run.

Back and Forth

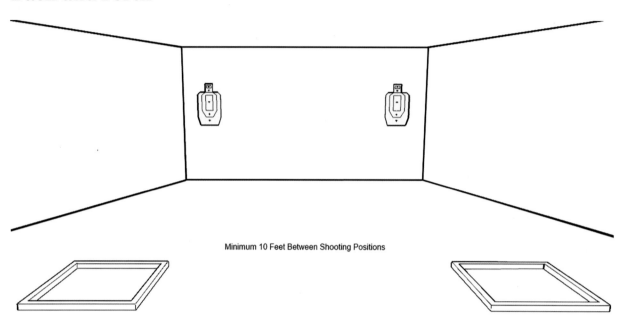

Minimum 10 Feet Between Shooting Positions

Date:	Notes:

Procedure:

Start on either the left side or the right side with any hand position you prefer. At the start signal, get a sight picture on the target in front of your shooting position. After the sight picture on the first target, move to the opposite position and get a sight picture on that target. Repeat this procedure back and forth for a total of four movements.

Focus:

Quickly set up in a position, get a sight picture, and then move to the next position.

Goal:

Gain the ability to get stopped, stable, balanced, and then explosively change directions.

Commentary:

This drill is similar in nature to "Skip Rope" that appears earlier in this section. This is a fun one, but you should save it for toward the end of a dryfire session because you are going to get very tired, very quickly, when you do this.

The instructions are simple; get set up on a sight picture and then get moving to the next spot. Repeat that four times, and then you are done. Of course, you can set a par time and work that down if you want, or you can just focus on the feeling of getting explosive direction changes off of a stable stance.

It is very easy to "cheat" on this drill by getting one foot into your firing position, and then waving the gun at the target and calling it good. You then move to the next spot and do the same. I recommend that you do not do this. Get set up into a wide and stable stance. You would want the ability to engage multiple targets from that stable position. You are only cheating yourself if you build bad habits.

Back and Forth Reloads

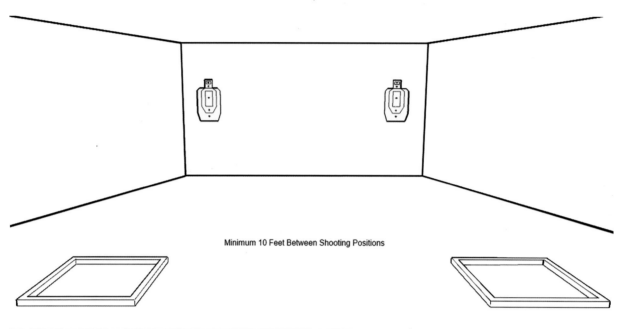

Minimum 10 Feet Between Shooting Positions

Date:	Notes:

Procedure:

Start on either the left side or the right side with any hand position you prefer. At the start signal, get a sight picture on the target in front of your shooting position. After the sight picture on the first target, move to the opposite position and get a sight picture on that target. Reload while you move. Repeat this procedure back and forth for a total of four movements and reloads.

Focus:

Quickly set up in a position, get a sight picture, and then move to the next position. Don't let the reloads slow you down.

Goal:

Gain the ability to get stopped, stable, balanced, and then explosively change directions while changing magazines between positions.

Commentary:

This drill is obviously very similar to the above "Back and Forth," with the added element of reloading every time you move. This is a good way to conceptualize it and a good way to train on it. You can certainly set a par time for this drill without reloading, and then attempt to match that par time when you add the reloads into the equation. This is very tough to do and a good challenge for you dry-fire session.

The big focal point here is to make sure that you still explode out of position and start heading to the next one right away. If you mess up a reload here and there, just shake it off and move on.

Part 8
PRACTICE STAGES

Designing your own dryfire practice stages is a great tool you can use to work on combining skills. What I am proposing is that you essentially take stages that you typically see at your club matches and build those same stages in your dryfire space. Obviously, you are going to be restricted in terms of how much space you have, but it can definitely be done. If you have something like a one-car garage, then you have plenty of space to construct entire stages for dryfire. You might need to be a little bit creative, but you can make it work.

What your focal point on long stages should be is clean execution over the entirety of the stage. On full stages, you might have to shoot 25 or 30 rounds, do a couple reloads, and change position four times. On top of that, you have a bunch of target transitions to do, along with needing to remember a target order and what positions to move to. For many people, especially new shooters, remembering all the things you need to do on a stage is a major challenge. Setting up practice stages and simply spending time training the memorization of the stage, then executing the stage plan without hesitating at all is a big deal.

For more advanced shooters, I think training on practice stages is helpful in terms of making sure your technique holds up as you string more elements together. It is one thing to do an explosive movement from one position to another if that is the only thing you have your mind on. It is quite another thing to do that same explosive movement when it is just one small part of a stage. It is a very helpful thing to execute training stages and just observe your technique. Make sure that you really are bringing out the best of your drill performance on training stages.

If you have a dedicated space for dryfire training, then there is absolutely no reason not to have a plethora of targets already set up and ready to go. You can simply designate targets and positions at random. Pick some group of targets to engage from one position and another group from the next. Keep going like that until you are satisfied with the stage. Then mentally rehearse the stage just like you would at a match. After that you can commence dryfire on the stage. It is best to make sure you pick things you aren't comfortable with! Work on backward movement. Work on seemingly illogical target sequences. These things pay off in matches when you don't get to dictate the skills required for the stage. The stage dictates what happens to you.

Of course, during dryfire stage practice you can set par times. It will take a few runs to figure out your par time, after that you can push down on the par time and try to improve your runs. As always, if you cheat on things, such as your sight pictures or grip, you are ultimately damaging your skills. Push to go faster, but make sure you are doing things properly.

There is much value to be had in this sort of training. Even if you don't have space at home to do it, then you should be doing it on the range. It doesn't take any ammo, and there is much to be learned.

Sample Stage 1

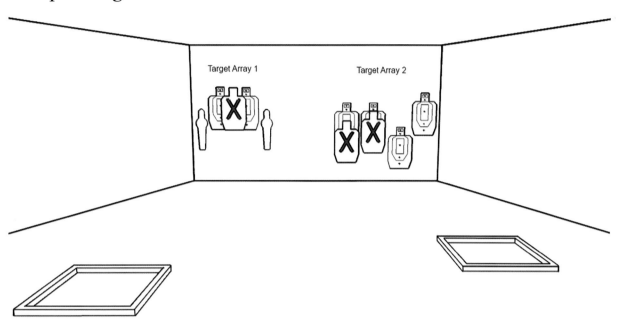

Date:	Notes:

On this stage, you can work with a few elements. The left targets can be taken from the left box. The targets on the right can be taken from the right box. You can work on position entry, position exit, hard entry, hard exit, drawing, reloading, and distance changeups. You could potentially run this stage in either direction.

Let me give you a few examples:

- Engage Target Array 1 from the left box, move to the right box and engage Target Array 2. Reload as you move.
- Engage Target Array 2 from the right box, move to the left box and engage Target Array 1. Reload as you move.

- Engage Target Array 1 from the right box, move to the left box and engage Target Array 2. Reload as you move.
- Engage Target Array 2 from the left box, move to the right box and engage Target Array 1. Reload as you move.

You can vary what direction you engage the targets within a particular array (left to right, versus right to left). You could engage the partial targets first, then the open targets. The possibilities are pretty much endless. You should work though all the skills discussed in previous drills in the context of a larger and more complicated stage.

Sample Stage 2

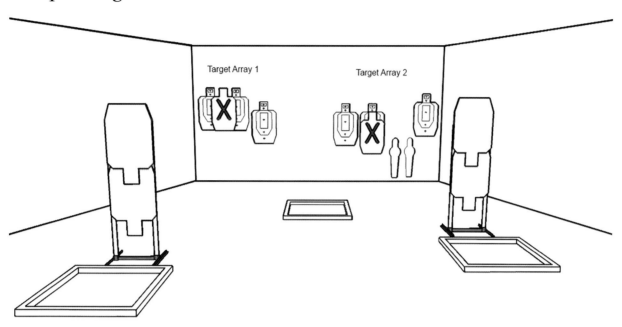

Date:	Notes:

As you can see, this stage has three potential positions to shoot from and two sets of targets. The possibilities here are multiplied immensely by the increased number of options.

You can vary the following things:

- What targets are engaged?
- What position the targets are engaged from?

- What order the targets are engaged?
- When are reloads performed?
- Do you shoot one-handed or freestyle?
- Do you engage from the left or right side of the barricade?

The possibilities are just about endless with a stage this complicated. The important thing is to zero in on the specific issues that you as a shooter need to work through. If you need to work on position entry, then skew the stage setup and procedure to emphasize that issue. If you need to work on reloading while moving, then work on those things.

Part 9
SAMPLE TRAINING PLANS

Many readers of this material will be wondering where to start. Do you work through the book in the order the drills are written? Do you work on the stuff you are bad at? How much should you train?

These questions are impossible to answer for everyone. You ultimately need to decide for yourself what it is you need to do. If you aren't "with it" enough to figure out what it is you should be training on, then you aren't going to be "with it" enough to do effective practice on your own without supervision. However, I have some ideas about what it is you should be doing and some sample plans you can use to formulate your own schedule.

The primary principle I use in my own training and recommend you use is that you should work on everything all of the time, and then put a special emphasis on the specific areas where you can benefit most from additional training. That means that everyone should continually train gun handing mechanics, trigger control, and long stages. If you are having accuracy issues at matches, then you should spend special attention on your trigger control. If you have a hard time remembering your way through stages, then you should spend additional time working on practice stages.

A good way to split things up is 50/50. This means you spend half your time doing the "everything all the time" practice. You work on everything in turn during that half of your time. A little bit of draw practice. A little bit of reloading. A little bit of movement, and so forth. During the other half of your time, you do very specific and focused training on the technical things that you feel you need to improve.

I think the 50/50 split should be done on a daily basis and not a multiweek basis. This means you shouldn't do the one drill you want to really master for a week straight all day, every day, and then spend the next week doing all the other things you want to do. That will be measurably less effective over time than doing that one drill half the time, every day, and the other things half the time every day. It reduces boredom and fatigue to continually be alternating between the drills you are working on.

Another thing that factors in here are specific goals that you have set. You need to read the drills carefully to understand what it is you should be getting out of them. For example, if you mean to move up in classification rapidly, then you will want to direct more effort to the standards section. If you are looking to move around better on field courses you need to work more with the scenarios section. Your long-term goals should drive a lot of your planning and preparation for competition.

With those basics in mind, I have a few sample charts I have prepared below. These come in four-week increments, and I have included basic instructions with them.

I have specified which of the five sections you should select a drill from for each day. On many days, I select two sections. Each practice session should last between 15 and 30 minutes. Spend about five minutes on each individual drill.

I have abbreviated the drill sections like this: (Elements: E) (Standards: STD) (Scenarios: SCE) (Assorted Exercises: AE) (Practice Stages: PS) (Day Off: OFF)

New Shooter

Week Number	Week 1	Week 2	Week 3	Week 4
Monday	E	E	E	E
Tuesday	PS	PS	PS	PS
Wednesday	E	E	E	E
Thursday	SCE	SCE	SCE	SCE
Friday	STD	STD	STD	STD
Saturday	OFF	OFF	OFF	OFF
Sunday	OFF	OFF	OFF	OFF

For newer shooters, I recommend focusing on training the basic elements. I have omitted the assorted exercises section for new shooters. It would probably not be too productive to mess around with that stuff just when you are getting started. Doing a bit of work learning to memorize practice stages would serve newer shooters well, and if they wanted to substitute in more practice stages training on the Thursday or Friday sessions, I think that would be totally fine.

Accurate, but Slow

Week Number	Week 1	Week 2	Week 3	Week 4
Monday	E	E	E	E
Tuesday	STD	STD	STD	STD
Wednesday	PS	PS	PS	PS
Thursday	STD	STD	STD	STD
Friday	SCE	SCE	SCE	SCE
Saturday	OFF	OFF	OFF	OFF
Sunday	OFF	OFF	OFF	OFF

For the "accurate, but slow" guys, I have placed an obvious emphasis on the standards. Those have very specific and measurable time limits, and quite honestly, you need to start pressing down on your par times. During your elements training (Mondays), you need to pay attention to those core mechanics. Get your draw faster! Reload the gun faster! Transition faster! Learn to shoot at the speed of your eyes. If you don't push, you aren't going to get faster, simple as that.

Fast, but Inaccurate

Week Number	Week 1	Week 2	Week 3	Week 4
Monday	E	E	E	E
Tuesday	PS	PS	PS	PS
Wednesday	AE	AE	AE	AE
Thursday	SCE	SCE	SCE	SCE
Friday	PS	PS	PS	PS
Saturday	OFF	OFF	OFF	OFF
Sunday	OFF	OFF	OFF	OFF

The fast, but inaccurate shooters need discipline. I would remove standard exercise training from the equation here, because having pie-in-the-sky goal times isn't going to improve the situation. Instead, the focus is on practice stages and scenarios training. During the scenarios training, work on seeing your sights for every shot and working the trigger straight. You absolutely should start to see your mistakes and where your poor accuracy is coming from and correct the problems. Do not chase even faster times if you are already fast, but not hitting anything.

Stuck In B Class for Two Years

Week Number	Week 1	Week 2	Week 3	Week 4
Monday	E, STD	E, STD	E, STD	E, STD
Tuesday	SCE	SCE	SCE	SCE
Wednesday	E, STD	E, STD	E, STD	E, STD
Thursday	E, STD	E, STD	E, STD	E, STD
Friday	SCE	AE	SCE	AE
Saturday	E, STD	E, STD	E, STD	E, STD
Sunday	OFF	OFF	OFF	OFF

The "stuck in B class" crew are people that tend to be too comfortable. I recommend doing lots of training on the elements, followed in the same day by getting hammered on the standards goal times. A smattering of other training rounds it out for these people.

Hardcore Training Plan

(Double the normal training, 30 to 60 minutes each day, broken into two sessions)

Week Number	Week 1	Week 2	Week 3	Week 4
Monday	E, STD, AE	E, STD, AE	E, STD, AE	E, STD, AE
Tuesday	E, PS, SCE	E, PS, SCE	E, PS, SCE	E, PS, SCE
Wednesday	E, STD	E, STD	E, STD	E, STD
Thursday	E, PS, SCE	E, PS, SCE	E, PS, SCE	E, PS, SCE
Friday	E, STD, AE	E, STD, AE	E, STD, AE	E, STD, AE
Saturday	E, PS, SCE	E, PS, SCE	E, PS, SCE	E, PS, SCE
Sunday	E or OFF	E or OFF	E or OFF	E or OFF

This is it . . . hardcore street. I recommend working on elements every single day of your training. This helps you constantly keep improving the core mechanics. Transitioning at the speed of your eyes, reloading and drawing the gun like lighting, and keeping stable when you move through positions. It is something you should be doing daily. You can then alternate days between pushing down on standard exercise times and refining your performance on long stages and shorter scenarios.

Part 10
DRYFIRE FAQ

Does This Really Work?

Yes, this works. Try it! Give it a real shot. Commit yourself to putting in some actual effort. You will see results, I can promise you.

How Do I Do Multiple Shots?

(This also appeared in "Part 2: Dryfire Logistics," but it is so commonly confused that it is printed again here, just to make sure you see it.)

With a **double-action pistol**, such as a CZ or a SIG, you should pull the trigger all the way (double action) for the first shot, and then not let the trigger out far enough for it to reset. For follow-up shots simply pull the trigger again. The trigger will not have any real resistance for the follow-up shots. When you reload or move from spot to spot be sure to pull your finger out of the trigger guard, your first shot after that will be in double action mode.

With a **single-action pistol**, such as a 1911/2011, you only get one pull of the trigger. The rest of the time you press back on an inactive (or "dead") trigger.

With a **striker-fired pistol**, such as a Glock, you can place a rubber band into the ejection port of the gun, with the goal of holding the gun slightly out of battery. If you do this appropriately, the trigger will not be able to release the striker, so the trigger will feel a bit squishy during dryfire practice.

With any of these pistols, you will be using the trigger differently than you would if the gun was being fired live. Unfortunately, there is no good solution for this. Focus on putting pressure on the trigger and directing the pressure straight back into the frame of the gun. If you can do that consistently, you will be well on your way to good shooting.

One thing that I think should be mentioned here is that when you are pressing a "dead" trigger, you should press the trigger *hard*. This provides a good simulation for how you will usually press your trigger during actual live-fire. When people are fighting recoil, the tendency is to press hard, so you want to simulate that tendency during dryfire and learn to press the trigger straight.

How Does the Timer Pick Up the Shots?

It doesn't. The function of your timer is to use the par setting. Consult the documentation that came with the timer to figure out how it works. The whole idea is to set the timer for the goal times and it will emit a second beep at the end of the drill.

How Do I Know If I Am Being Accurate or Not?

Watch the sights carefully. You need to bring some understanding of what the sights should look like at any given distance in order to score good points. If you don't know how precise of a sight picture you need to hit the "A" zone, then figure that out in livefire. When you get to dryfire, you need to hold yourself accountable for the sight pictures that you see. If you aren't sure whether you had the required sight picture, then consider it a miss.

In short, you know if you are accurate or not based on your livefire experience. You need to hold *yourself* accountable to that standard.

There are some devices on the market that are designed to assist you. The most popular among them are the laser-emitting devices that you can insert into your gun. There are even the SIRT pistols designed to emit a laser pulse with every press of the trigger. These devices can be problematic for practical shooters. If you are training yourself to have a sight focus, then the laser dot being emitted on the target can be a real distraction. You can certainly use the laser to supplement your regular dryfire, but I don't know anyone that puts up with the distraction of the laser over the long term. Eventually, you need to learn to accurately read the sights yourself.

How Much Better Than Dryfire is Livefire?

It is very common for people to believe that livefire training is superior to dryfire training. They think livefire is more effective. In many ways, this is true. In other ways, it isn't.

I think livefire is a valuable and necessary tool. You get the feel of the gun going off. You learn to track the sights. You can see how much the gun bucks around when it fires. You get used to the muzzle blast. There are many sensations you need to be acclimated to

in order to shoot at the highest level. You also need feedback. You need to put holes in targets and figure out how to make the holes be where you need them to be. You need to confirm your dryfire training is working.

In many ways, you don't need to shoot real bullets to get the same impact in your training. For example, when you are doing draws, you are working on building up your grip of the pistol. You are perfecting bringing the pistol up to your eye line with the sights aligned. You are bringing all of those little technical elements together. There is no part of any of that where you need to fire a round. It simply isn't part of the equation. So, in that respect, dryfire isn't any worse than livefire.

The point here is that you should abandon the idea that dryfire practice is good, but livefire is better. They are both important. They can both help you. There are advantages to both in different scenarios.

You should avoid the mentality that livefire is better than dryfire. Both of them are serious training. Both of them can take you places. If you adopt the mindset the livefire training is better, then I feel like you will neglect your dryfire training. That would be a poor idea.

Why Am I Almost Always Slower in Livefire Than I Am in Dryfire?

Figuring out exactly why dryfire times are faster than livefire times is a widely discussed question. Of course, the obvious answer is to point to the fact that the gun is recoiling when you shoot live rounds and the recoil recovery time constitutes the time difference between livefire and dryfire times. I think it is certainly accurate to point to recoil as one factor, but there is a plethora of other issues that come in to play. I don't have the data at this point to figure out exactly how each of these factors affects your times, but you should understand that instead of one issue, there are a constellation of possible issues.

One important thing to remember is how the level of tension in your body during your gun manipulation will affect your times. Generally speaking, people move fluidly and precisely when they feel relaxed. I have often experienced my body tensing up when I get out to the range to shoot "for real." I have observed this same phenomenon in other shooters as well. That additional tension often produces mistakes that add time to draws and reloads.

Another thing to consider is that the motion in the sights can make people slow down their shooting. I consider this to be separate from recoil control. Many shooters are able to hold their guns on target during rapid fire shooting, but are unable to read the sights fast enough to take advantage of it. Of course, during dryfire the sights will remain stable because the slide isn't flying back and forth to chamber fresh rounds. With training, this issue can be minimized or even totally overcome, but for newer shooters it can have a devastating effect on stage times.

Finally, many shooters aren't honest with themselves about the quality of their sight pictures during their dryfire. This leads to extremely fast dryfire times and then inconsistent livefire results. Frequently, someone with this issue will end up unable to "shoot fast" when they are actually on the range. They end up slowing everything down just to make sure they don't miss targets completely.

GLOSSARY

"A": The maximum point-scoring zone on a USPSA target

Dryfire: Practicing with an unloaded firearm

Grandbagging: Attempting to obtain a classification that is above your "true" skill level

Group shooting: Shooting a few shots in the same place on the target

Hosefest: Stages that do not have demanding marksmanship challenges

IDPA: International Defensive Pistol Association

Index: Ability to look at a spot and have the sights show up in alignment on that spot

Limited Division: USPSA division defined primarily by allowing everything except optics and compensators

Livefire: Actually firing a gun

Open Division: USPSA division allowing for significant modifications to the competition firearm including optical sights.

Production Division: USPSA division using predominately unmodified firearms

Sandbagging: Attempting to remain in a classification that is below your "true" skill level

Sight focus: Having your optical focus on your sights

Splits: The time between shots

String: A number of shots at a target or group of targets

Strong hand: Your dominant hand

Super squad: The group of the top shooters at USPSA Nationals

Target focus: Having your optical focus on the target you are engaging

Transitions: Moving the gun from one target to another

Trigger freeze: Attempting to pull the trigger so fast that you don't pull it far enough to discharge the gun

Walkthrough: The stage inspection period at a match

Weak hand: Nondominant hand

USPSA: United States Practical Shooting Association

ACKNOWLEDGMENTS

Special Thanks:
I would like to thank guys like Brian Enos, Saul Kirsch, Mike Plaxco, and Rob Leatham. Each of them, and many more, have contributed in some way to this book and my development as a shooter, and they deserve credit.

Testers:
The following people (along with some others) tested the concepts in this book, and also provided content feedback.

Andreas Yankopolus
Hwansik Kim
Matthew Hooper
Matthew Hopkins
Brian Hansen

Dave Solimini
Patrick Scott
Randy Lopes
Tim "Full Timmy" Mcycrs

Editing:
Ronnie Casper once again edited the book. The book would not be possible without him.

Illustrations:
Ronnie Casper contributed all of the diagrams.

Photography:
Beyond Photography provided the photos. Additional photos were provided by Tim Meyers.

OTHER TITLES WITH
SKYHORSE PUBLISHING

Breakthrough Marksmanship
Ben Stoeger
120 Pages
ISBN: 978-1-5107-7936-5
Price: $15.99

Practical Pistol
Ben Stoeger
216 Pages
ISBN: 978-1-5107-7948-8
Price: $24.99

Practical Shooting Training
Ben Stoeger, Joel Park
336 Pages
ISBN: 978-1-5107-7934-1
Price: $29.99

Adaptive Rifle
Ben Stoeger, Joel Park
144 Pages
ISBN: 978-1-5107-7946-4
Price: $24.99